5-HOUR MBA

The Business Owner's Guide To Success

CHAD REINERTSON

Summit Venture Group publishes its books in a variety of electronic formats. Some content that appears in print may not be available in electronic books. For more information about Summit Venture Group products visit our website at www.5hourmba.com.

ISBN-13: 978-0692-64150-7

ISBN-10: 069-2641-505

Printed in the United States of America

PREFACE

Three years ago, I wrote *Don't Start Your Own Business* as a complete step-by-step guide to actually help entrepreneurs start and run a successful business. I wanted to share my knowledge, hardships, challenges and successful strategies I had learned along the way building my five startup companies.

So I did what I felt would make the greatest impact, and was brutally honest about the difficulties creating and running a company. I still believe it's not for everyone. If I can save you from wasting thousands of dollars and sleepless nights, I will.

You must have a strong desire, a unique blend of stubborn openness and sometimes reckless disregard for reality to be a business owner. My desire to see young businesses succeed motivated me to write that book.

I spoke directly to the problems I knew other entrepreneurs had, and I had witnessed first-hand. Problems that I have experienced myself, along with actual solutions I used to overcome those challenges and succeed.

Since that first publication, online marketing has gone through a major growth and evolution. Content marketing and email automation have become vital in marketing today, and changed the way companies interact with customers. Social marketing and SEO strategies have also taken giant leaps forward, to become a major force driving online traffic and lead generation.

These strategies are so important, and changing so rapidly, the information I provided in *Don't Start Your Own Business* needed to be updated. Every month brings a new story and discovery.

This is not a revised edition because the original principles don't work. They absolutely do!

This is a major update to include current technical marketing practices and tools to keep your business on the cutting edge. This edition contains 60 pages of NEW content and strategies from CEOs, executives, professional marketers, business owners and entrepreneurs and tested in real-world situations.

5-Hour MBA is a completely modernized guide to help you start your own business. While many of the fundamental core components for building a solid foundation remain, I have added all new sections on the latest digital marketing strategies and industry secrets from professionals.

Today, I'm the CEO of Uproar Group Marketing. My team creates highly focused online content marketing campaigns and builds fully automated sales funnels. Seeing first-hand the power of quality content driven marketing, I'm a firm believer in startups investing time and resources into these areas. They are critical to building a successful business in today's market.

The lessons presented in this book are much more than theory. They have been confirmed through thousands of hours split testing, monitoring, tweaking, testing again and seeing success. This book goes way beyond case studies and theoretical what-if's. These are real steps and results that you can duplicate, from real people.

Running Uproar Group Marketing, I have learned an immense amount. Digital marketing has become my life and I'm surrounded by it every day. I have spent years studying, analyzing, implementing, testing and critiquing each of these strategies I present.

Not to mention talking with other CEOs, business owners and industry leaders about their stories and strategies. This is as much a collection of their pain points and solutions, as it is mine.

Millions of business owners continue to struggle with these challenges. This book addresses the most important aspects of running a business and covers what you need to know.

You may be asking yourself, is this book for you? Will it really help me and my business? The answer is yes!

From studying, building and running businesses for over 15-years I can tell you the principles presented in *5-Hour MBA* are shared by every single successful company!

It was also my goal to share important insider tips and latest tricks to help build your business faster and get ahead of your competitors.

I have received lots of great feedback and questions from readers over the past few years. Here are some common questions I get asked most often -

Q: Does my business already need to be successful in order to take advantage of these strategies? No.

Q: Do I need a large marketing budget to implement the campaigns you're talking about? No.

Q: Do I have to change my business plan? Absolutely not.

Q: Do I need to be a tech savvy 20-year old to understand technical marketing? Not at all.

You don't need to have a business background to use the lessons taught in this book. In fact, it's written for all backgrounds and knowledge levels. You don't need an ivy league education to understand the principles taught here and apply them in your business.

My objective is to create a resource and guide for everyone to use, no matter their situation or background. Certain commonalities exist in business, and this guide shows you how to apply them in your company to see real improvements.

If you're nervous about starting your own business, struggling to launch a new company, not sure if you'll make it another year or want to take your business to the next level – this book is meant for you.

Do you ever wonder how some business owners seem to have it all figured out? They're flying off to the Caribbean or taking family vacations to Thailand, while you're grinding out 12-hour days and can't imagine leaving your company for a month.

They're not better a business than you. They simply understand the same secrets and principles for building a modern company I'll show you in this guide.

I want you to avoid the same common mistakes that I've made and see others make way too often. I want to help you turn your idea into a reality faster, launch your product more successfully, get your company off the ground and make your existing business more profitable.

You can spend tens of thousands of dollars on an MBA, spending late nights and long hours away from your family, and come away with the same knowledge presented in this book. I've been there. Sacrificing my personal life, time with family, fun with friends and activities that made me happy...to sit in a classroom with a group of 30 other people I barely knew.

While the lessons they teach in the classroom are valuable, it's more valuable understanding how and when to apply them. Which principles truly work in the real world and which ones are more academic. When is the right time to apply this lesson or execute that strategy?

I'm 100% confident, following the steps and lessons presented in *5-Hour MBA* will help you start and run a successful business.

Visit our site and creative laboratory www.5hourmba.com for the latest information, courses and expert advice for achieving your business dreams.

ACKNOWLEDGEMENTS

I want to thank everyone who helped make *5-Hour MBA*, and the original edition *Don't Start Your Own Business*, possible. Writing this series has been a dream of mine for a while and it would have been much more difficult without your support, encouragement, and inspiration. I would like to thank Matt and Jaime (my business partners) for their priceless teachings, Linda and the entire Westminster MBA program, Joanne (my tireless copy-editor), Jon (my brilliant legal advice), Mark, Brittany, Ryan and Richard for their valuable input, my MBA classmates for driving my creativity and keeping me sane all those late nights: Jeff, Vladamir, Brian P, Alex, Courtney, Dylan, Nadia, Kelli, Brian H, Amie, Jessica, Jesse, Sean, Alex & Diane, and finally to all my long-time friends from Luther College. My journey started there. Thank you for everything you've been part of.

I would especially like to thank Emma. Your motivation, ideas and encouragement pushed me to create the 5-Hour MBA program. You are an inspiration.

To my mother:
Thank you for your inspiration

To my father:
Thank you for your innovation

To my sister:
Thank you for your determination

Contents

FORTUNE FAVORS THE BOLD

~ Virgil ~

DON'T START YOUR OWN BUSINESS

THE INTRODUCTION

So you have an idea that's going to be the next great thing. Everyone's going to want one and you'll sell millions. Just one problem....you have to start your business first. Each year thousands of people just like you face the same realization. How do I turn my idea into a reality? Should I start my own business? Where do I begin? What do I need to know in order to be successful? How do I manage my business better? I'm here to give you a real look at what it takes to start a business, launch your product and build a company able to compete in today's world.

This is your complete and easy to follow step-by-step guide to walk you through the entire startup and growth process. The lessons presented are much more than theory taught in MBA programs. They have been confirmed through thousands of hours of testing, monitoring, adjusting and testing again. This book goes far beyond the classroom and simple case studies. These are real strategies you can duplicate, from real business owners, to build your company with. I'll detail common challenges you'll face and mistakes you need to avoid. Most entrepreneurs have to learn the hard way usually costing them valuable time and money. This practical guide gives you the information and resources you need to know in order to avoid such costly mistakes. The difference between success and failure will be the choices you make. This book will give you the knowledge you need to make those decisions.

The best advice I can give you is to *not* start your own business. It's painfully frustrating, exhausting, costly, and will affect the relationships you have in your life. You will dedicate everything you have to it without any guarantee of a return or a pay check. You can expect to work long hours, late nights, have uncertain outcomes, make plenty of mistakes and add stress in your life. But, if you are one of those people determined to live the American Dream and build your own company, then this guide will help you.

I started my first business when I was 24. I was terrified to take that leap and had no idea where to start. I knew what I wanted to do, but had so many questions about how to begin without completely messing everything up. Since then I've started four more companies and earned my MBA. I've been a small business owner for the past 15 years. While my MBA degree was helpful, it didn't provide all the answers for running a competitive business I needed. In the process of all this I've made my share of mistakes and learned many valuable lessons. My goal is to share those stories along with the insight and education I've picked up along the way from hundreds of other executives, MBAs and business owners, so you don't have to learn the same hard lessons I did.

As a small business owner you'll experience the highest of highs and the lowest of lows, often within the same week. I'll give you the tools and knowledge to help you not only survive, but thrive. Through these simple, proven, and streamlined steps you'll gain valuable information about running your own company that successful business owners have used for years. I'll also give you insider secrets to help you get ahead of your competition. Trust me, they don't want you to know this stuff.

The previous belief that 90% of small businesses fail in their first year simply isn't true anymore. Technology and resources available to startups have improved significantly. More information is readily available. It's cheaper and easier to reach customers than it was several years ago. The truth is there are more startups and small businesses than ever before, and the majority of those are making it past their first year. That's the good news. The bad news is only about half of those companies make it past five years. Running a business will be difficult, confusing, and frustrating. The business landscape is constantly changing, even from just a few years ago when I published the first edition of this book, and it's tough to keep up. You'll make a lot of mistakes along the way that will cost you both time and revenue. Ultimately how big or small your mistakes are will determine your success.

Through the years of running my own startups, I've faced countless challenges that I have been able to overcome with these key core strategies and lessons. This book is a collection of the most successful practices taught by top MBA programs, used in real companies and confirmed with actual results.

This book cuts through the basic theories and provides a complete guide of real steps that you can follow. I want this to be a resource that helps all small business owners with useful information and sensible practices. Not only to launch your product, but also to improve your business and manage it more effectively so you'll survive and succeed. There's no absolute right way to start a business but there are wrong ways.

During my early years, I looked for answers to my many questions by reading dozens of books, online blogs and articles. I found they mostly provide theories and discuss optimal situations; ideas that work really well if you have unlimited funds or extraordinary resources at your disposal. Many books focus on great success stories like Walmart or Coca-Cola. While these are great stories, my personal marketing budget and business approach are a little different than Walmart's. As entrepreneurs, our resources are much more limited and valuable. We need a guide that shows us how to be successful in today's business world, with what we have using proven strategies.

I've spent countless hours sorting through the endless mess of information, searching online for useful answers, only to be frustrated with my efforts. My desire to write this book comes from wanting to share practical advice and vital lessons to help those struggling with a startup.

In this book I detail how to get started, when to spend money, when to hire professionals, and when to do it yourself. Knowing how to maximize your resources are some of the most important decisions you'll make. I'll give you real solutions to common challenges business owners face. You're not going to avoid every problem, but I'll give you enough information to be prepared when they do arise. Avoiding the costly mistakes will be the difference between success and falling into the traditional hardships of owning a small business.

I'll also give you specific steps to run your business more effectively, generate higher quality leads, drive more traffic to your brand, compete against larger companies (and win) and increase your sales using real practices from professional marketers. I'll walk you through some of the most important marketing strategies every company needs, and explain how to attract more customers than your competitors.

So, if I can't talk you out of leaving that nice cushy 9-5 job with a 401(k), guaranteed salary and PTO, and you're convinced starting your own business is the best thing for you, then good luck and let's begin. Welcome to the world of being an entrepreneur!

1

WHO NEEDS AN MBA?

The Lessons of Business School

I got my MBA a few years ago and it was the best thing I ever did. But you don't need a degree to start a company or create your product. I had been running two of my businesses for five years before I decided to go back to school. However, the information, resources, and techniques provided in my MBA program were vital to improving my strategies and achieving greater success. I'll share those lessons with you.

My background was never in business but I knew that I needed to take my companies to the next level. Everything I knew about running a business was learned from on-the-go experience. My decisions were more reactive than proactive. I would make a mistake, fix it, and simply try not to make it again. It was the wrong way to operate, because the day-to-day operations were time consuming. I missed a ton of opportunities, forecasting was impossible and failed to attract repeat buyers. I was working hard to keep up rather than making decisions to anticipate trends and put me ahead. I didn't have a formal understanding of how to run a business and make better decisions. For five years I struggled to keep up. I was doing just enough to keep my doors open, but each week was a grind. I wanted to be on the other side of the 'hump' but didn't know how to get there. So I made the decision to take on an enormous amount of school loans and selected a top ranked business school in Salt Lake City, Utah.

During the course of my MBA program, I went through almost everything there is to running a business. I say almost everything, because you'll experience things in business they don't teach you. These are the real-world lessons we'll get into later. I found, in business school, there are several core concepts everything is built upon. These core concepts are absolutely valuable and key to operating a successful business. The rest, in my opinion, is filler to support these core ideas.

5-Hour MBA covers each of these core ideas taught in a professional MBA program. This is a comprehensive guide of those strategies, giving you the same knowledge and information with the added guidance of how to execute each strategy for the best results. MBA programs fall short teaching students how and when to implement these lessons in their business. This book details proven methods to use each core MBA concept to help your business succeed.

I've implemented these practices into my own businesses and utilize them every day now. I'm going to weed out the academic fluff and get right down to important information. I'll spend the next several chapters detailing each fundamental lesson from business school and building the right framework for your startup. By the end of this book, you'll have learned the same lessons taught in a full MBA graduate program.

If you are just beginning and still in the development stage, this is a necessary foundation. I urge you follow each step presented. If your business is already established, or a startup, compare these ideas and practices to your own. You'll find valuable lessons to increase revenue and take your business to the next level. Here's your complete guide to having an MBA.

PRODUCT

What are you making? What are you selling? Product is what everything else revolves around. It is what your customers are paying money for. Your product needs to add value to a current need or demand. This is the most important point I can make. Your product must offer a value to the customer they're not already getting from any other product. Your value can be price, function, form, speed, entertainment, or any number of things. As you start this process, ask yourself this very important question. Does my product add value? Does my product offer a benefit over other products currently out there? You can have the flashiest commercials, coolest packaging, and the most expensive marketing campaign, but it won't mean anything if your product doesn't add value. Customers won't buy it and your business won't last long. What is your value?

First things first. You need to know what you're getting yourself into. Start by researching all the products in the market similar to yours. Look at what they're doing and why they're doing it. Products that are already in the market can give you a lot of information about your customers, the market, trends, and strategies. Get to know everything you can about your target market before you start anything else. This is called a Market Analysis. It will completely describe your specific market and competitors. Its important information will greatly influence your decisions when designing and launching your own product. Gain a clear understanding of the products currently meeting customers' needs. After completing the Market Analysis, if you still believe your product offers a real value and benefit over current products, then you might be on to something.

Let's start your Market Analysis by making a list of your competitors and competing products. We're going to make three different lists to analyze competitors. Fill out each of these lists and keep them as part of your Simple Startup Guide. This book will walk you through various exercises that you'll continually refer to. Organize them in a convenient location that you easily refer to throughout the process. The first table is a basic look at major competitors and what they offer. We call this the 30,000' view. What companies are competing in the market? What is their value compared to your product? You want to get a very basic idea of who they are, what they do, and how they operate.

30,000' VIEW

	COMPETITOR #1	COMPETITOR #2	COMPETITOR #3
General Business Model	What industry are they in? What do they do?		
Competitive Advantage	What is their focus that makes them better than others?		
Strengths	What do they do well?		
Weaknesses	What do they not do well?		
Market Position	Are they high end or economic? Customized or mass marketed?		
Products	What do they sell?		
Target Market	Who are their customers?		

The second table is a <u>Breadth and Depth Chart</u>. This goes into more detail about the number of products they offer versus what you'll offer. This table breaks down individual products they are selling to clearly illustrate their market reach and strategy. For example, if your competitor sells their product in every color, except for red, then why not? Is it too expensive, not enough demand, or not good quality? This analysis will show you either opportunities or barriers. Maybe you designed your product only in red and need to look more into it, or maybe you developed a cheaper way to make a quality red product and can immediately fill that need. I've filled this in with an example for a clothing company competitor.

BREADTH AND DEPTH CHART

DEPTH (colors, styles, sizes, features)	PRODUCT #1 Shirts	PRODUCT #2 Pants	PRODUCT #3 Hoodies
Men's	Styles, sizes	Cuts, designs	Colors, zipper vs. non
Women's	Styles, sizes	Cuts, designs	Colors, prints
Child	Prints, logos	Elastic waist	Movie characters
Winter	Long sleeve	Snow pants	Heavy duty no zipper
Summer	Short sleeve	Shorts	Light weight full zip

The third table is your <u>Competitor Profile</u>. This gives much more detail to analyze their operations. How are your competitors making money and what sales channels are they using? What is their strategy and advertising to drive sales? It will give you a clear picture of their strengths, weaknesses, and strategies.

COMPETITOR PROFILE CHART

	COMPETITOR #1	COMPETITOR #2	COMPETITOR #3
Sales Channels	Storefront, Local outlets, online, wholesalers		
Revenue	Price, transactions, subscription, volume-based		
Partners	Who do they partner with?		
Target Market	Who are their customers?		
Advertising	Where do they reach customers?		
Branding	Colors, icons, customer recognition		

Communication	Press releases, emails, newsletters, blogs		
Income Model	Instant, waiting period, credit		
Operating Costs	Overhead costs		
Sales Methods	Salesmen, advertising, online		
Success Factors	What is critical to their revenue?		
Barriers	What challenges do they face?		

You can find all the information you need on the Internet. Online resources are the easiest ways to research competitors, find customers, and get a clearer understanding of your market. It wasn't long ago that most of this research had to be done at libraries and was both time consuming and painstaking. Depending on the library, they may not have had the information you were looking for. Now search engines return results within seconds and there is a wealth of information available online. Be careful of your sources when researching competitors and always look for trusted sites. But you will have no problem finding plenty of information to complete these worksheets with a few online searches. It's one of the greatest tools small business owners have available to them and one of the reasons startups are lasting longer.

Here are several helpful websites to find market information:

BUSINESS RESEARCH RESOURCES

US Bureau of Labor Stats	www.bls.gov/csxhome.htm	Consumer Stats Database
US Census	http://www.census.gov/ces/dataproducts/bds/	Market Size & Demographics
Demographic & Lifestyle Info	www.segmentsolutions.nielen.com/mybestsegments	Regional Demographics
EDGAR SEC Filings	www.edgar-online.com	Public comp. market share
BPlans	www.bplans.com/industry_reports/categories	Industry info and reports
Bureau of Economic Analysis	www.bea.gov	Industry and Regional Stats
Media Finder	www.mediafinder.com	Index of media outlets
Other Good Sources	www.factfinder.census.gov www.makemypersona.com www.quora.com	Market categories and information

SWOT ANALYSIS

By now you should have a clear picture and solid understanding of the market you are getting into. You should know who your competitors are, what their products are, how they position themselves, and how they make money. Now we're going to focus on your product by completing both a SWOT and Market Analysis. SWOT is one of the most common terms you hear in business school. It stands for Strengths, Weaknesses, Opportunities, and Threats. A good SWOT analysis will point out what competitive advantages and opportunities you have in the market. You will also use it in your overall marketing strategy. Get used to hearing this term and thinking of these four factors as your company grows. I recommend that people perform a SWOT analysis each month to be aware of any market changes or new opportunities. For your Market Analysis, we're going to dive deeper and look at several key market forces that will impact you. The Market Analysis explores some of the underlying factors influencing your marketing strategy. After completing these two exercises, you will know exactly where your product falls in the market and your position.

SWOT ANALYSIS

STRENGTHS	What is your appeal? What makes your product better than other products? What do you do better than your competition?
WEAKNESSES	What are your product limitations? What internal limitations will prevent you from succeeding?
OPPORTUNITIES	What external opportunities exist that you can take advantage of? Untapped resources, new market, new technology, or trends.
THREATS	What external limitations will stop you from succeeding? Competitors, other product substitutes, or regulations.

Did you see some unexpected results in the SWOT analysis? This gives you a clear picture of what you're doing well and what you need to focus on. This basic information will help shape your overall marketing strategy we're going to work on shortly. Next, let's complete the Market Analysis and examine market forces in your industry. What drives and shapes your industry? What influences how companies in your market do business? Understanding these forces are key to operating smoothly and efficiently.

For instance, if you manufacture a food product and spend months getting everything ready to launch in grocery stores, then the FDA informs you that your product requires FDA approval and will cost thousands of dollars plus months of testing. Imagine how detrimental that is to a small business with weekly overhead costs and a limited budget. Unexpected setbacks will happen to you. That's just a fact of life. Accept that they will happen and be prepared to deal with them. However, the more research you do before-hand will greatly help you avoid major delays and improve your ability to get into the market quicker. Let's get started.

MARKET ANALYSIS

MARKET FORCE	INFLUENCE
POLITICAL / LEGAL	Political regulations, legal restrictions, registrations, requirements
TECHNOLOGY	Acceptance of technology in the market, commonly used systems, rate of change
CONSUMER	Consumer buying trends, behaviors, market size, buying power, expendable cash, price points
ECONOMIC	Market health, unemployment percent, job growth, spending power, industry growth
COMPETITIVE	Barriers to entry, competitors, cost of entry
EVENTS	Holidays, festivals, natural disasters

Unexpected market forces can be very costly and time consuming to a small business. Spend a little extra time examining what's going on, and perform a Market Analysis annually. It will help save you a lot of effort in the long run.

Congratulations! You just completed your first semester of business school. Right now you've got five pages of tables and analysis. Keep this in your Simple Startup Guide. This is the information you need to successfully position yourself in the market. You know who your competitors are, what they're doing, and what the market looks like. You also know what your value, strengths, weaknesses, and opportunities are. Now it's time to develop your own position and marketing strategy.

THE WHEEL HAS BEEN INVENTED ALREADY

You don't need to come up with a unique idea or create a completely new product. Most products that are introduced into the market are adaptations of other existing products. Take a look at Apple for example. They are rarely the first ones to the market with a new product. Smart phones, MP3 players, and tablets already existed before Apple introduced their iPods, iPhones, and iPads. They simply created products that added more value to customers. They were cooler, smaller, had new features, multiple colors, easily synced together, and gave the customer something different. Apple didn't try to reinvent the wheel. Instead, they added more value to products in a growing market. Look for ways your product can add more value too.

2

SUCCESSFUL POSITIONING

It Determines Everything

Positioning involves making critical decisions about your **Product, Pricing, Promotions, and Placement**. These are called the four P's and will absolutely determine your success in the market. It determines whether a customer sees your product, understands its value, accepts the price, and ultimately buys it. The four P's are the foundation of every sale. Spend time to really think about these when you're starting out. These decisions can change as the market evolves, as you grow, and as outside factors affect your operations. Coco-Cola, Disney and Apple adjust their pricing and promotions on a regular basis, and go through these steps each time. It's critical to get started right, because you may not have a lot of resources and capital that allow you to experiment with these items. Most startups have a limited amount of time to get launched, so getting the four P's right the first time is important.

PRODUCT

It's time to get down to the fun part and think about your product. There are some important decisions you'll have to make right away. You may already have a product in development, a proto-type, or even a finished product. At a minimum, you have an idea of what you want to make. Here are some important topics to consider:

- **QUALITY** – A basic goal in business is to reduce your operating expenses while maximizing your revenue. You want to make the largest sustainable profit possible. Quality is often the first factor that gets examined and adjusted. How are you going to make your product, where are you going to make it, what materials are you going to use? What do your customers demand for quality and what are the risks of altering your quality? When choosing the quality of your products, look at the risk versus reward. Think of the customers you're selling to and the market you're selling in. Are you competing with high-end shops or on an economic level? Make smart decisions that meet your standards and your customer's standards, fit the market place, deliver a decent margin, and ultimately will sell your product.

- **DESIGN AND STYLE** – Let's face it-we're attracted to good looking products.   Design is one of the factors that can give your product added value. There's no clearer example than the iPod. When Apple introduced the iPod there were plenty of other MP3 players out there. But the iPod was cool with a different style and flashy colors. As consumers, we're drawn to products that look good and create an emotional reaction. Cool cars, hot clothes, elegant jewelry, and sleek computers. Apple was able to jump to the forefront of MP3 player sales with their style and design. Now think about what makes you unique. How are you different from your competitors? Consider how important this is in your market and how design drives sales.

- **LABELING** – This may seem as simple as slapping your name on a label, but it's actually more complicated than that. Many industries have strict labeling requirements. Manufacturers are required to follow regulations and provide specific information on their labels. Food products are a great example with their label requirements. Everything must have the same format with calories, ingredients, vitamins, and minerals. Different countries will also have their requirements for labels. Cosmetics sold in Europe are required to print ingredients, batch numbers, testing codes, and warnings which are quite different from cosmetic label requirements here in the United States. Research label requirements before you start designing them. This can be another costly and time-consuming mistake that is easy to overlook.

- **PACKAGING** – By the time you finish reading this, you've already lost the customer. You only have a few seconds to grab the customer's attention and bring them in. Packaging is the first thing consumers see and must create enough curiosity for them to look at your product further. Close your eyes and imagine this. You are in a grocery store walking down an aisle. There are literally hundreds of products to choose from. What catches your eye and why do you pick it up? You read the label, then flip it over and read the back. It looks good, so you buy it. Everything is determined by the packaging. Now, can you remember the other similar products you passed by? Probably not. As a business owner you have a split second to draw the customer in, convey your message, and make the sale. Your packaging must be interesting, clear, uncluttered, and create a feeling of confidence for the customer. It's a good idea to test your packaging before finalizing the design and ordering everything. Get a group of 20 friends and family together. Have several different package designs along with a few competitors. Line them all up and ask your friends to rank them. Record their feedback on what they like and what they didn't. These reactions are going to be the same as your customers will have. So take some time to find the right packaging. It's worth spending extra money to get the right design. The right look will draw consumers in and be worth it in the end.

- **CUSTOMER SERVICE** – You'd better have it. I can't make that any clearer. We're going to get into how important good customer service is a little later on. When thinking about your product, consider how much customer service will be required. Is it leading edge technology that people will need training on, will you process a lot of exchanges, or will parts need to be reordered frequently? Customer service is the foundation of longevity-plain and simple. Create a plan for how much customer service your product will require. If it's too much to handle, then you need to either adjust your product or your business plan. Let me warn you-failure to provide adequate customer service will come back to hurt you. To illustrate this, just think about an experience where you had great customer service and one where you had horrible customer service. How did both experiences make you feel and how likely were you to reorder from the company with the bad experience? Plus, how many people did you tell about your bad experience? Word of mouth travels quickly, especially with technology today. One bad review can wipe out 10 good reviews. You are already facing enough challenges with this startup, so don't create more for yourself by decreasing consumer confidence. Come up with a good customer service plan and stick to it.

- **BRANDING** – Welcome to one of the most complex challenges you'll face. It's tough to describe, it's hard to figure out, and there are no formulas. We can spend days discussing branding, and we'll definitely dive deeper into this. For right now, we're going to strip it down and make it simple. When I say the words "Nike Swoosh", what do you think of? There you go...that's branding at its best. Two words invoke visions of Nike's symbol, their slogan, their mantra, their products, athletes who wear it, and probably a dozen other things. That little symbol encompasses who they are, what they do, what they stand for, and creates consumer confidence. That's branding. The consumer can see one image and doesn't need to be told anything else. It's part of the ultimate goal you're chasing.

- **LIFE CYCLE** – I have not met many small business owners that think about this. Product life cycle includes four stages of your product development.

  Introduction - When your product is first launched and starting to make sales.

Growth - When you start to expand into more markets, customers become more familiar with your product, and profits start to rise.

Maturity - When growth starts to decline and sales tend to level off. Typically, this is when other competitors introduce substitute products similar to yours.

Decline - When your sales are declining either due to lost interest in the market, a change in economic forces, or too many similar products. Your product life cycle is important to think about while forming a sales and marketing plan. Is your life cycle one year or ten years? How long will it take you to reach other markets and how long will it take competitors to introduce a similar substitute product? If it's easy for competitors to make a good substitute, then you'll need to be more aggressive with your marketing plan. On the other hand, drug companies, for example, can block substitutes of their products for years allowing them more time in the growth stage. Consider your life cycle now before we get into writing a marketing plan.

- **BREADTH & DEPTH** – See, I am tying back in those previous exercises you did. You have to make decisions about your own product line that work for your resources.

How many product lines do you plan to have and are they necessary to create your competitive advantage? I talk with a lot of small business owners who believe they need to have multiple products simply because their competitors do or because they want to hit more market segments. This actually puts them at a disadvantage starting out. Having more product lines will require you to have more resources. The limited capital you do have will be spread thinner. Instead, consider starting with a few core products. Look for specific niches your competitors aren't in and get a feel for the market. Startups need to be very careful with their resources, so you need to develop a smart product line strategy. Plan out your breadth and depth that will make you the most competitive in your market.

PRICING

This sounds like an easy one at first glance. My competitor is charging $20, so I'm going to charge $19. Don't get caught in that trap; consider pricing more carefully. Your competitor may be more established or have other market factors going in their favor. Consumers can be very price sensitive and there a lot of market factors that go into setting your price. We've all driven the extra mile just to save a few cents on a gallon of gas. We've also all paid more to get a product we're familiar with instead of a competitor's less expensive product. Pricing doesn't need to be complicated, but you do need to have a good strategy. We're going to focus on the strategy behind setting the right price, how to actually calculate your price, and when to use discounts.

Write down each of these topics below, along with your answers. This will shape your pricing strategy. As your company grows you'll refer back to these any time you adjust your pricing.

- **OBJECTIVES** – What end result are you going for? Do you want to be the low price leader, viewed as exclusive, or simply a good price for a great product? All three of those require different pricing strategies.

  Low price leader - requires you to monitor competitor prices and continually adjust yours to be below theirs. Several large stores have used the phrase "low price leader" as their slogan. They are very clear on their pricing strategy and what they're going to do.

  Exclusive - infers from the basic supply and demand graph that you'll be a higher price. Exclusive models, exclusive events, and exclusive brands require you to keep price higher than the market average.

Intrinsic value - perceived by the lack of supply and therefore can charge a higher price. There are many market factors that play into this outside of just setting your price high, so you need to be aware of these. The last example actually uses more of an independent pricing strategy.

Independent pricing - put your product out there at a price you set. It's above the lowest and below the highest priced competitor. You're not as concerned with competitors pricing. You are justifying your price with the quality or value of your product. This is what most business owners do. Determine your objective and that will influence how you set your price.

- **STRATEGIES** – Pricing strategies determine how competitive you are in the market and ultimately your revenue. Sell too low and you may not make enough. Sell too high and you may not sell anything. Prices can fluctuate throughout the year based on supply, demand, or market factors. Good pricing strategies combine competitive prices with the right timing. Some of the most effective strategies I've seen have been dynamic to also capitalize on changing market forces. What forces dictate the pricing in your market? What can influence or change it? Examine different pricing strategies for your market that take advantage of events or trends during the year. Pick the strategy that maximizes your profits and gives you the greatest competitive advantage.

One important item of note is you'll see the terms revenue *and* profit *moving forward. It's important to distinguish between the two, because they have very different meanings. Revenue refers to the total amount of sales or income you make. This is before any costs or taxes are taken out. Profit is the amount remaining after you remove your costs, expenses, and taxes. It's the money you take home. It's very easy to have high revenue and $0 profit. This reflects that your costs are high. Be aware of the difference between profit and revenue as we start to mention them more.*

ONE PRICE, TWO PRICE, THREE PRICE, FOUR

One of the most interesting examples of pricing strategies I've seen comes from a ski resort in Utah. They introduced a dynamic pricing model to coordinate pricing with demand. They offer different pricing in multiple sales channels based on anticipated demand. First, they offer local retailers three different pricing tiers. Level 1 receives a small discount for their customers, level 2 a bigger discount, and level 3 an even bigger discount. Next, the resort sells lift tickets online directly to customers with a dynamic pricing calendar offering a certain number of tickets at various prices through-out the year. A family of four may be offered two tickets at $70 and two tickets at $90. One day later, all four tickets may be offered at $85 each. Prices continually change based on the number of tickets sold. The resort also offers a third pricing model to wholesalers and travel agents. Finally, the lift ticket window has a fourth price for walk-up customers. Their dynamic pricing strategy allows them to set and maximize lift ticket prices in 4 different sales channels. Since introducing this price strategy, this ski resort has increased their profits. Disney also uses dynamic pricing at their parks, selling tickets at a 4% discount to 20% increase based on daily visitors. Uber and Lyft utilize price multipliers based on demand that can increase as much as 500%! These are complex strategies most of us will never use, but illustrates how unique and important pricing is.

- **DISCOUNTING** – SALE! SALE! SALE! We've all seen these signs and it's a powerful emotion when we think we're saving something. Some businesses resort to putting up huge banners reading "Limited Sale" all year long. Using discounts creates a greater sense of urgency to purchase based on a belief we won't get that lower price later on. We don't want to miss out on that price, and drive us to purchase immediately. Discounting also reaches customers outside your target market. Consumers place a value on every product that's equated to a price. When the right price is reached, they'll buy it. Discounting needs be planned carefully, since it can also have negative effects on your revenue and image. At the lower price, customers may think your product is a lower quality or cheap. If your goal is to be exclusive, then discounting to a lower price may damage that exclusive image. If you discount often enough, customers may not buy products at full price again and, will expect a sale price. Determine the frequency and amount you discount based on your market and events.

As an exercise, walk through your local mall and notice how many retailers advertise sales or discounts? How do they advertise the sale, is it a special event, and how much is the discount? Next, evaluate the effectiveness of the sale. Does the discount make you want to buy? Make a list of each sale you see and rank them in order of effectiveness. What qualities do the top sales share and what makes them successful? Then consider applying these same properties to your sales plan.

TWIST MY ARM

If you're not familiar with the outdoor retailer Backcountry.com, look them up. I use them in several examples, because they do a lot of things really well. I believe many small businesses can improve their own operations by looking at ideas and strategies Backcountry.com uses. Backcountry.com has a sub-branded site, called steepandcheap.com, used to sell a variety of outdoor products at discounted prices. Here's the twist – they sell one product at time, discount it heavily, and add a timer when the sale expires. This sale usually lasts between 10-15 minutes! They do a phenomenal job creating a sense of urgency to purchase right now. Strategically displayed is the quantity remaining and time remaining. The emotional reaction of possibly missing out on that sale instantly drives the buying experience. Seeing there is only one left instinctually twists your arm to buy it now. Companies are always searching for ways to engage the consumer and urge them to purchase immediately. Steepandcheap.com accomplishes this incredibly well. It's the reason why I personally own four tents and three sleeping bags from them.

- **TARGET MARKET** – I hear so many people say, "Well there are 74 million people in this market and I'm going to capture 1% of them." No, no, no, no, no! I can't stress this enough and we'll talk about this again in developing your sales plan. Your target market does not encompass everyone out there. You need to really look at things, like age groups, economic standing, income, buying power, education level, and influencers (religion, marital status, community leaders) when deciding your price. Break down your market and look at what

potential customers are really in it. You can rank
them based on a scale from 'likely to buy' to
'definitely will not buy.' Focus your pricing strategy
on the consumers most likely to buy. Let's do quick
Customer Profile exercise to identify specific
categories of buyers within your target market.

CUSTOMER PROFILE CHART

GENDER	
AGE	
EDUCATION LEVEL	
GEOGRAPHIC LOCATION	
INFLUENCERS	
SPENDING POWER	
TECHNOLOGY USE	(low/ medium / high)
ECONOMIC CONDITION/HEALTH	

Now you have a better idea of who your customer is. You can have 10 of these Customer Profile charts if necessary. Make sure you know this information before going any further. Simply stating I'm to capture 1% of my market is a red flag to fail. Create a detailed Customer Profile analysis and put this in your Simple Startup Guide.

- **COMPETITIVE PRICING** – I had a professor in my MBA program that told me once, "You'll know when you're successful, because you'll have lots of competitors breathing down your neck-so you might as well get used to them." There are very few scenarios where you'll be the only company in the market and can set whatever price you want. The United States has anti-trust laws to try and prevent this. The reality is you're fighting competitors for the same customer and price will influence them. So get used to using competitive pricing. It's a key factor for any customer making a purchase. Your price needs to be competitive, so customers don't automatically dismiss it when shopping. You can have a higher price, but your value needs to justify that to the customer. Setting it too high, or low, risks losing that customer. Do research on similar product prices, secretly shop competitors, and regularly map out where your pricing stands in relation to other similar products. The price you set has the ability to separate you from the competition either positively or negatively. Adjust the price as necessary and even run a sale if it helps grab the customers' attention.

To help illustrate where your pricing places you in the market or where you should be pricing your product, create a simple line graph. Draw a straight line with $0 on the left end and a maximum price ($100, $1000, $10,000) on the right end. Place each of your competitors and their prices on this graph. Then place yourself on this graph. Where do you fall on it? Is this where you want to be?

- **PRICING METHODS** – There isn't one single right way to set your price. You already know your target market and what competitors are charging. Seems simple from there to set your price, but who said this would be simple? There are four methods to calculate a price that will help maximize your margin.

METHOD	DESCRIPTION	EXAMPLE
VALUE-BASED PRICING	Set your price based on the product's value to the customer. This method can often return the highest margin.	Your new fuel additive saves the customer $50 in gas each month. Even at $40, it is worth it to the customer who is happy to save a net $10 per month.
COST PLUS PRICING	Add together your product costs, cost of goods, fixed costs, and margin to set the price. Provides consistent margins given your costs are correct. Beware of increasing costs.	Your gift baskets contain $30 cost of goods and cost another $30 to make. You want a 20% margin for $12 (20% x $60). Your price is $72 per basket.
TARGET RETURN PRICING	This is based on the capital you have invested, the rate of return you want, and the rate of sales. Calculates the price you must charge to meet your revenue goal.	You invested $100,000 and want to make that back in one year. You expect to sell 1,000 units in that first year. Each unit costs $50 to make. $100,000/1000 units = $100 margin per unit plus $50 cost = $150 price to make $100k in the first year.

CONSUMER PRICING	Customers will decide how much they feel a product is worth, regardless of your production cost or added value. Effected by changing market conditions and common in the market place.	Back to the fuel additive. It saves customers $50/month in gas. They feel $40 is too expensive for an additive and will only buy it under $20.

- **TERMS** – I generally tend to stay away from offering pricing terms, but you may be required based on the customer, market, or your competition. "Terms" simply mean offering something other than the normal 'pay the one price upfront' model. Sixty days same as cash financing, half now half later, lay away, payment plan, subscriptions, volume discounts, COD, and payable upon receipt are all various payment terms. If you find that competitors are offering payment terms to customers, find out why and what the risk-versus-rewards are. If you determine that need to offer them also, make sure to fully research what you are offering. Otherwise, keep it simple and collect payments up front.

You've noticed by now that many of these topics tie together which reflects the strength of a good plan. Your pricing plan will support your marketing plan that will support your sales plan. These all weave together to form a complete working strategy. I hate when authors get repetitive, so I'll do my best to avoid redundancy while making the points clear. On to more **Positioning** and talking about **Promotion**.

PROMOTION

How are you going to get your message out there and reach customers? You can have the greatest product in the history of mankind and it won't mean a thing, if nobody knows about it. Promotion is all about where and how you communicate your message. It is picking the most effective channel to get your product out there and in front of customers. There are literally hundreds of ways to do this. Do a quick online search for 'promotion ideas' and see how many are returned. In my search I counted 265 different ideas just on the first search page. The good news is there are tons of free ideas. The bad news is this can actually hurt you, if you go after too many of them at once. You have to decide which promotional ideas are going to benefit you the most, bring in the right customers, fit your branding, and maximize your profits.

More important than how you promote is how you communicate your message-how you say it. The best advice I can give is to be honest and make the message personal. Consumers respond better to a personal connection they can make with you. They need to feel confident in your product and can sniff out gimmicks pretty quickly.

Next, take a look at customer perceptions in the industry versus your value proposition. What do customers think about current products in the market? What do they want out of those products? Your message needs to address the customer needs and while differentiating yourself at the same time. Then it's about finding a way to reach potential customers with that message. That's where Promotion comes in. I'll break down a few of the time-tested methods and teach you how to pick more effective promotion ideas.

- **OBJECTIVES** – As with *Pricing*, we need to determine our objective at the start of picking the right *Promotions*. There are several main objectives, based on what product life cycle you're currently in. This will play a major factor when deciding your goal. Is your product new and trying to build awareness? New products need to establish an identity in the market before customers start buying. Are you pitching your value and creating interest? As we talked earlier, customers need to see the value before they buy and this is where promotion comes in. Are you advertising the value of your product? Other promotions are simply to provide information for customers. This can help strengthen market position or increase awareness, without actively pursuing a sale. Is your goal to make sales right away and actively drive the customer towards a purchase? This can be sales, discounts, pre-holiday ads (avoid the rush before the holiday), special events, or trial offers. Promotions can quickly turn a shopper into a buyer. Or are you simply trying to stay in touch with the customer after the purchase? Companies keep in touch with customers through newsletters or blogs to reinforce the relationship. Next time the customer is ready to purchase; they'll think of you first. Develop your objective and the right promotion will be easier to pick.

- **BUDGET** – As a business owner, you will always struggle with how much to spend on advertising and promotions. I'll show you some formulas you can use to help estimate the Return-On-Investment (ROI). However, chances are you don't have unlimited resources and you'll have to make some tough decisions on how much to spend. Don't spend enough and you may not reach enough customers; spend too much and you may be wasting it. The key is how much should you spend to get good results without over leveraging yourself? Many small business owners set a percentage of revenue for the amount they'll spend. This is a safe method that gives you flexibility, won't single-handedly break your bank, and will grow as your sales do. As you're starting out, 10% of your revenue is a common amount to budget for promotions. Begin there and track the results for several months. If you're not seeing the penetration rate or return you'd like, then examine adjusting the percent. Also, if you're seeing great results from spending 10%, consider increasing it slightly to see if the returns also increase at the same rate. Be smart and creative with promotion ideas and really stretch the budget as far as you can take it. There are lots of free marketing ideas we'll discuss later that will help maximize your ROI.

• **RESOURCES** – Remember when I said, "Network, network, network." This is the topic I was referring to. Reach out to your network of friends, family, and neighbors to see who may work for a television station, magazine, or distributor. Utilizing people, you know is one of your best resources. For one of my first start-ups, I had three business partners. We were really on a tight budget and scrapped together every contact we could find when it came to promotions. We were really surprised how far it got us. One of my partner's next-door neighbors is a vice president at Nordstrom's department stores. My second partner lived next to a general manager for 67 health spas throughout the west. He happened to be looking for products similar to ours and arranged one of our first big wholesale purchases. My third business partner went to school with the host of a highly rated morning TV talk show. Just between my immediate partners we had enough contacts to arrange free promotions and opportunities in our market. Look beyond the usual resources, like paid advertising, that cost money. Those are costly and will burn up your capital quickly. Search for more personal resources you have available and can utilize. You'll be surprised what you find.

- **INTEGRATED MARKETING STRATEGY** – Sounds like something a Navy SEAL team would devise. It's not that scary. Integrated Marketing Strategy simply means combining traditional media outlets, like television and newspaper, with new technology resources, like social media and online communication. You want to leverage multiple communication tools to hit consumers from several angles. Keep driving your message in different shapes and forms. You also want to allow for feedback from your customers. Development of social media and blogs, where you can get real time and direct interaction with your customers, is dramatically changing how we develop Integrated Marketing Strategies. I'll detail what tools are readily available and various promotion resources you can combine when we discuss the marketing plan. Start thinking about various channels that make sense to combine or already work together-like how blogs, social media, and television can be blended together and support each other. Using only one or two promotion ideas really limits your reach and effectiveness. Develop a multi-layered promotion plan that builds upon each other to maximize your message.

- **TARGET MARKET** – By now you've heard the term target market enough that you can recite exactly who they are in your sleep. Great. Now what do they respond to? How do you get them to listen to your message and what kind of promotions will grab their attention? This is how your promotion objectives and Integrated Marketing Strategy come into play. Do you see how this is all weaving together? You need to create an effective message that grabs your customer's attention. You can shout all day long in the middle of Manhattan and not get one new customer. You need to promote where your target market is and you need to have a message they'll listen to. Think about what influences your customer. What information are they looking for? What affects their life? Find where your target market gets their information from. Is it TV, magazines, social media, blogs, friends, or newspapers? This can be as simple as asking members of your target market. Ask them where they go when they shop? How do they pick out a product? Get feedback from current customers too. Set up questionnaires through blogs, online forums, social media, emails, or mailers that gather information about how customers shop. I'm sure you've all seen the little drop-down question in the online checkout page of 'how did you find us.' That little question gives you results on what channels your marketing is driving, how effective your spending is, and where you should focus more efforts. You need to be smart and effective with your budget, so don't waste it on areas your target market is not in. Collect data that you can use to narrow down your scope and make your strategy more effective. Ask the questions and you'll get all the answers you need.

POP QUIZ

You have a new line of great wrinkle removing cosmetic products. You want to tell every woman with a wrinkle or age line about it. You want to promote to any woman who even thinks she sees a wrinkle. Which channel can you find a high percentage of your target market in and reach them directly?

A) television commercial during a cooking show
B) print ad in a women's magazine
C) online forum for new mothers
D) partner with a local health spa

Answer: Online baby blogs and forums' highest percentage of users are women ages 25 – 45. They are actively discussing new products, changes in their life style, and providing other users with reviews on products they like and don't like. Many of them are also early adapters of new products or technology. Most of these forums are free to sign up for and provide a wonderful opportunity to communicate directly with your target market without spending a dime. Several of these blogs reach more of your target audience than high price paid television does.

- **MESSAGING** – Once you've reached your potential customers, make sure that you have the right message. Many small businesses can have a hard time with this. Larger corporations pay professional firms a lot of money to create specific messages that resonate with customers. Your message needs to be on topic, clear, concise, and communicates your value proposition. Remember, consumers aren't as concerned with the details of how great something is as they are with the benefits it gives them. A sports car driver doesn't care that your car has 240 horsepower (hp). He likes that the 240 hp can accelerate him from 0-60 mph in under three seconds. He likes the feeling and sound. You need to create a message that quickly communicates the value proposition and what makes your product unique. First, think of what differentiates your product from competitors. Then, list the benefits customers will see in their life because of those unique attributes. Instead of saying our new vacuum is two pounds lighter than the competition state the benefit that it is easier to carry up and down the stairs. Focus on finding the right message customers will respond to.

Think about a simple acronym F.A.B. to help you remember this point.

> F – Forget about *Features*
>
> A – Avoid selling *Advantages*
>
> B – Customers buy *Benefits*

- **MEASUREMENT TOOLS** – Technology today makes it easier than ever to measure customer response, interaction, and marketing penetration rates. Google provides free analytics when you register your Google account (also free) and web domain with them. Google Analytics allows you to measure unique visitors, how customers use your site, how they got to your site, sales, visit duration, bounce rates, and conversion rates. They provide free reports on Social Analytics, Mobile Analytics, Conversion Analytics, and Advertising Analytics-all reports, tracking, and information you need right at your fingertips and all for free. Simply do an online search for Google Analytics to find these great resources. There are so many readily available free metrics and reporting tools.

Facebook, along with most social media sites, provide detailed analytics measuring the success of your posts. They provide free demographics about your target audience and reach. Learn to utilize the free tools available to you. There are even several inexpensive paid analytics tools such as Microsoft Power BI that consolidate numerous metrics on to one easy-to-manage dashboard. A quick online search for 'marketing metrics' provides hundreds of results for free measurement tools. You can track and view consumer behavior quite easily now.

These reports are extremely useful to determine the success of your *Product, Pricing, Promotion,* and *Placement* decisions. The numbers show you everything from bounce rate (how many customers leave your site after the first page) to visitors by region. You'll be able to see, in real time, consumer response to your actions. The numbers will tell you if you're on the right track or need to make improvements. Having a high bounce rate over 60% says that customers aren't seeing the value in your message and you need to improve it. Utilize these free measurement tools on a daily basis. Understand why spikes and dips happen, use them to predict trends in the market, and get a clear picture of how consumers respond to your decisions.

PLACEMENT

Our fourth and last P is *Placement.* This determines where you place your product in the market place, how you manage that placement, and any impact outside forces have. After all the research you've done so far, you should know exactly where your customers shop. This will help determine where you place your product. Resources also are a big determining factor. Small startups may not have the capital to rent out high priced store locations, so are forced to find placements that fit their resources. Think about longevity when considering placement. How much does it cost for you to be in that sales channel, what are the results, and how does it affect your image? You want to be able to be in a market long enough for consumers to get to know you and recognize you. What I'm saying is don't spend all your money on prime placement for one month, hoping it's going to take off. Placement will always take longer than you expect. Pick two or three channels that you can sustain for a year. Experiment with those and refine your business plan as you go. If your product adds real value to consumers, you'll see it in sales. Don't make the costly mistake of forcing yourself into the wrong placement simply because you see competitors being successful. That's a sure fire way to burn through capital.

- **CHANNEL TYPES** – You would have been lucky to start your business 20 years ago when there were only two types of sales channels-brick and mortar or wholesale.

Now retailers are selling through many more options. Sales channels come in many shapes and forms. You can break them up into direct and indirect. You'll most likely use a combination of both and that's encouraged. It really depends on your customers for which one you focus more on.

Direct Channel Types
- o   E-Commerce site
- o   Online retailer
- o   Pay-per-click ads
- o   Facebook page
- o   Print ads
- o   Online ads
- o   Store location
- o   Door-to-door sales

Indirect Channel Types
- o   Blogs
- o   Forums
- o   Affiliate marketing
- o   Newsletters
- o   Contests
- o   Public events

First, decide the best way to reach your target market. If you have your own e-commerce website to sell through, then you are already selling directly. The cost of starting a website today is incredibly affordable. There are thousands of website templates to choose from that you simply paste in your content and pictures. Direct marketing gives you the most control over the content and design.

Indirect marketing typically relies more on consumer participation or third parties to work well. Affiliate marketing can be a powerful indirect marketing tool when you're getting started. Chances are you don't have too many sales channels established at this point. Affiliates have established sales to similar audiences. Partnering with them can open up new opportunities and actually sell product for you. Almost all affiliates charge upfront fees and take a percentage of your sales. A prominent, influential affiliate can have enormous impact on your sales, especially starting out and still trying to establish your brand awareness. Select affiliates carefully that have a strong following, similar customer attributes and will positively impact your brand image. Make sure it's a good deal and works for your plan. Indirect marketing can be very powerful to help drive sales, while allowing you to focus on your direct marketing at the same time.

- **CHANNEL INTENSITY** – This simply refers to the number of competitors and substitute products already in your market. How many options do consumers have to choose from? Ultimately, you'd like to choose a segment with fewer substitutes. It allows you to offer a greater value and differentiate yourself. Next time you're at the grocery store, stand in the cereal aisle and look at how many similar options there are sitting right next to each other. Channel intensity will affect your price sensitivity, package design, marketing plan, margins, and profit. The more jam packed a market is, the tougher it is to differentiate yourself. From your research you already know how many competitors are in each market. Start out by looking for markets with fewer competitors or adjust your messaging to separate yourself from the main pack. Find opportunities to go after the low hanging fruit.

- **PARTNERS** – Tiffany & Co. doesn't sell their diamonds in K-Mart. You have to find the right partnerships that add value to your product. Be selective in seeking out the right partnership that can add mutual value. Putting your product in the wrong stores can devalue your product and give the wrong message to your customers. Don't pass on less-than-perfect opportunities, but, if it doesn't make sense, then don't do it. When you do sign a partnership with either a store or affiliate marketing company, be

aware of the placement they are giving you. Being buried
on the 10th page or bottom shelf may not help you.
Working with the right partners to promote your product
and drive sales will make a huge difference. Don't be
afraid to negotiate on placement either. They will either
tell you they can do it or what it'll take to get there. Always
make sure you are picking the right placement and
opportunity for your product.

- **TRANSPORTATION METHODS** – I'm just going to mention
this quickly, because I've seen startups make this mistake.
Consider the time and cost involved in shipping your
goods. I know a spa product retailer in Minnesota who
signed an agreement to sell his products in a southern
California spa chain. At first, he was elated over the
additional sales channel. When he started to make regular
shipments each month, he realized the variable costs of
shipping ate into his margin. When gas prices climbed, his
costs increased, but the retail price stayed the same.
Finally, as gas prices continued to rise, he had to cancel the
contract, because he was losing money on the deal. Take
into account transportation costs. Ensure you are getting
your product delivered on time, safely, securely, and at the
right price. Look for opportunities closer to home where
you can control the shipping methods better.

- **CHANNEL MANAGEMENT** - Very few business owners understand what this term means. Sales Channel Management is simply a process for marketing, selling, and servicing customers in each channel. Think of it as the complete journey for your customer's experience. From beginning to end, what steps do you have in place to keep things running smoothly, have the product delivered on time, prevent issues, and keep the customer happy? First, set your goals for what you want to happen in that channel. Do you want on time delivery, enough products in stores, or keeping a low inventory? Next, ensure your process support the customer needs. Remember, this isn't about you...it's about your customer. <u>Manage your channel to fit your customer's needs!</u> Design a quick questionnaire to see if you're actually meeting their needs. What can you do to make their buying experience better? Don't underestimate the impact being out of stock, late shipments or decreased quality for faster production time will have on customers. Establish policies and practices ahead of time to avoid potential problems. Establish policies that will ensure everything runs smoothly. Every company has customer service policies, return policies, and management policies. Good channel management keeps your product moving off the line, out your doors, through the store, and into the customer's hands smoothly. It keeps everyone happy.

- **BUYING PATTERNS** – I often think that mindreading is easier than predicting consumer buying patterns, but, with the help of today's analytics, it allows you to dial in to how customers are behaving. Correctly interpreting those analytics will give you a good of idea of what people are looking for and what entices them to buy. Look at all the customer data that you've collected. What messages are resonating with your customer, what trends are going on, what economic conditions are either driving or stopping economic growth? This is all information available through the free analytic reports. You just need to understand how to look at it. Examine your page bounce rates and see which pages visitors are spending the most amount of time on. Those pages have the most interesting information or message that visitors are curious about. Where are the friction points in your website or buying process? Look at trending topics on social media or the highest searched phrases to monitor trends. News channels report on economic conditions every day. Learn to use the numerous free resources all around you. Then, put yourself in the consumer's shoes and imagine what's important to them. This helps you establish a buying trend.

When the United States economy takes a dip or falls into a recession, General Mills' stocks go up. Why is this? Because more people stock up on the food products General Mills makes. Buying patterns change every day. However, if you are able to detect or predict those patterns, then there is a wealth of sales for you to make.

This concludes the overview on *Positioning* and the four P's. **Product, Promotion, Pricing,** and **Placement**. How do you feel about it? This is your foundation, so make sure you understand it. We go into much more detail on these topics in upcoming chapters, plus use this information when building your actual sales and marketing plans. This information becomes critical to forming solid strategies that actually work. A lot more goes into making sales than just throwing your product out there and waiting for the customer to come along. That's called fishing and it relies on luck. Successful businesses rely on a strategy and *Positioning*.

3

CREATE A USEFUL BUSINESS MODEL

Because Mission Statements Are Pointless

Seriously, when was the last time you heard someone rattle off their mission statement? Truth is they're outdated and not many people use them anymore. More useful to you is a solid business model and that's what we're going to build. A business model should be really simple. How are you going to make money? That's it. If you don't know how you're going to make money, then you won't. That's the focus of what we're going to create. All of the other questions that go into building a successful business model you've already answered.

- Who is your target customer?
- What is the problem with current products?
- What is your value?
- Where will you find potential customers?
- How will you reach these customers?
- How will you differentiate yourself?
- What is your cost and profit margin?

- How will you generate revenue?

This is all the information that goes into writing a business model. It is a road map that shows you how you're going to make money. Let's start with where the money's going to come from.

Here is a little secret that will really help you to get your business launched, not only with your sales, but also when you're pitching to investors. Don't assume you're going to capture a certain percentage of the market and all those people will buy your product. Investors hear that all the time and it's a sign of someone who doesn't know their market very well. Instead, identify your first 10 customers. How are you going to get your first 10 sales? Who are they? Where are they? How will you reach them? Write that down, focus on that plan, and explain that to investors. I shake my head when someone tells me they're going to capture 1% of their market. No, you won't. Start with your first 10 customers, tell me how you're going to reach them, then tell me how you're going to reach the next 100 customers, and then the next 1,000. That is a more educated and realistic business model. You'll not only stand out to investors but you'll get more sales starting out.

You can either write your business model or organize it in a chart. We can make a chart similar to the Competitor Profile you did in chapter 1. This time you're going to fill the information out for your customers.

BUSINESS MODEL

TARGET CUSTOMER	Who are they?
CURRENT PROBLEMS	What's the problem?
VALUE/DIFFERENTIATION	How does your product solve that problem?
CHANNELS	Where are your customers?
PROMOTIONS	How will you reach your customers?
PRICING/REVENUE	How will you make money?
PLACEMENT	Where will you sell your product?
PARTNERS	Who will you partner with?
OPERATION COSTS	What costs will be included to produce, market, and sell your product?
PRIORITIES	What is important in your operation?
KEY FACTORS	What can make or break you?
CASH FLOW	How often do payments come in versus going out?

Keep your business model simple and realistic. It doesn't need to be lengthy; it just needs to be complete. You should be able to explain what you do in one sentence. If it's confusing to you, then the customer won't understand it either. Write out the answers to the questions above. Who, where, why, and how? This is your map that will hold you on course, so keep referring to it.

How do you feel so far? By now you know who your customers are, where they shop, how to reach them, what value your products bring, your market structure, and your business model. Are you clear on how you'll make money? You are either feeling more confident about your product or a little less excited than you were.

Relax, this is normal when you start to lay everything out and see the details. Do you still feel your product adds unique value and that you can reach potential customers with your message? How does your business model look? Do you know how you're going to reach your first 10 customers? Are you making as much money as you thought you would?

DECISION TIME

This is a good decision point. If you still believe your product brings a unique value to the market and you can reach customers, then you are ready to move forward. If you're not so sure, then go back and re-evaluate your idea, sales channels, positioning, and business model. From here on out you'll spend money and have capital invested. You'll also spend an enormous amount of time working on the startup. If you're still on board, then get ready for the adventure that's about to begin.

4

START YOUR COMPANY

Build It The Right Way

Y ou've made it to the point of actually starting your company. Congratulations! You should feel good about your decision. I'll give you an easy to follow step-by-step guide to help make this process easier. First, you need to decide what kind of company you want to start. How you organize your company now will impact your operations, taxes, and regulations. You have several options for the type of company you want to start. We'll go through the most common options, along with tips for setting it up right. I realize many of you may have already started a business and completed this set up process, so you can skip ahead a little or read through this to ensure you organized your company the right way.

Here's my recommendation to you: hire a qualified attorney or business professional to set up your business classification. This is worthwhile to spend money on. They can provide valuable advice on which one will benefit you the most. It's so critical to get your business set up correctly. There are many online services that offer to do it cheaply, but leave room for error. Hiring a local attorney or professional is a cost that's worth paying. Getting the right help from the start will benefit you in the long run. As you start to file taxes and create financial statements, you definitely want to have everything filed correctly. A business attorney will help you choose the correct business classification, file the paperwork and ensure you are protected. Spend the money to hire a good professional and do it right. This is one area you don't want to leave open to chance.

There are four main types of companies you can choose from:

- **Sole Proprietorship**
- **Partnership – general or limited**
- **Corporation – regular or S Corp**
- **Limited Liability Company (LLC)**

The purpose of selecting the right business organization is to protect you from risk and liability. You must also consider how certain classifications can affect your ownership rights, like tax liabilities, partnerships, and income. Each type of business has various legal requirements. Which type you select will determine those requirements and how you operate. Laws can be very specific on what you can and can't do based on the type of business you choose.

SOLE PROPRIETORSHIP - A sole proprietorship has a single owner. All the control and responsibility rests with that owner. It allows decisions to be made quickly and with greater flexibility. You can form a sole proprietorship fairly simply and easily. You also have some excellent tax and saving advantages such as a SEP IRA that allows you to save up to 25% of your earnings up to $53,000. That's considerably higher than traditional IRA contribution limits. However, you are responsible for raising all the capital, liability claims against the business, claiming all of the business's profits on your individual tax return, and filing all correct licenses.

GENERAL PARTNERSHIP - This is formed between two or more people as co-owners of the business. The percentage of ownership can be flexible, based on your arrangement with the other partners. Profit sharing will be determined by that agreement and each partner's ownership percentage. A partnership is also fairly simple to set up by a professional. Company liabilities are shared by all partners and can be extended to your personal assets. Partners share in the profits or losses and then report those amounts on their individual tax returns.

LIMITED PARTNERSHIP - Similar to general partnerships, limited partnerships allow for silent or limited partners. There must be at least one main general partner that manages the company.

Each general partner will share in the full liability amount. The limited partners are not required to contribute in the operations and their liability is based on the percent of their investment.

CORPORATION - A corporation is made up of shareholders, has its own rights, and liabilities are separate from the owners and individuals. Corporations must file Articles of Incorporation, declare to be either for profit or non-profit, pay taxes on the company profits, and require more in depth records. Shareholder liability is limited to the amount or percentage the shareholder owns. Profits are distributed to shareholders as dividends that get reported on each shareholder's individual tax return.

S CORPORATION - An S Corporation is a combination of both a partnership and corporation. "S Corps" are allowed to have up to 100 shareholders. The IRS allows them to pass all profits or losses onto the individual shareholders in order to avoid paying corporate taxes. The shareholders then report their percentage of profit or loss on their individual taxes. Thus the S Corp does not pay taxes itself, except in special situations, such as excess net passive income or on certain capital gains. "S Corps" can only have one class of stock issued to shareholders, must be made up of individuals instead of other corporations, and are regulated as regular corporations are.

LIMITED LIABILITY COMPANY (LLC) - LLCs are also a combination of partnerships and corporations. LLCs are made up of members taking a predetermined percentage of the company, although they must file Articles of Organization. LLCs are managed directly by the members or elected managers. LLC's profits may be taxed either as a corporation or passed to the members to report on individual tax returns, based on the setup. LLC's separate the members from direct liability.

STATE LICENSES AND REGULATIONS

Don't forget to file with your state either. You'll need to obtain a state tax ID number and also a local business license. If you operate a physical location, you'll need to file with your city and obtain certain insurance policies. The list of local requirements can be lengthy so again a qualified attorney is incredibly valuable to walk you through the steps and paperwork required. Spend the money to get the right advice and file everything correctly the first time. Even one missed form can result in a costly penalty. You can find out more about your state and local requirements by contacting your Chamber of Commerce or state's business division. To find these do a simple online search for government services.

	Proprietorship	General Partners	Limited Partners	Corporation	S Corp	LLC
Creation	Owner starts operating	Partnership agreement	Partnership agreement	Article of Incorporation	Articles of Incorporation	Articles of Organization
Owners	Single owner	Multiple partners	General and limited partners	Shareholders	Shareholders	Members
Liability	100% liability	Partners share in full liability	General partners share in full liability and limited partners are based on investment	Shareholders liable only for capital invested	Shareholders liable only for capital invested	Members have limited liability
Control	Owner has 100% control	Partners determine percent of control	Controlled by general partners; limited partners have no rights	Shareholders elect board of directors to operate company	Shareholders elect board of directors to operate company	Members and elected managers control operations
Capital	100% from owner	Received from partners, may be unequal amounts	From both general and limited partners	Sale of stock	Sale of stock	Contributed from members
Taxes*	Income Tax, Self Employment Tax, Social Security/Medicare, Federal Unemployment	Employment taxes, income tax, self employment tax	Employment taxes, income tax, self employment tax	Income tax, employment tax, excise tax	Income tax, employment taxes, FUTA, depositing employment tax, excise tax	Employment taxes, income tax, self employment tax
IRS Forms*	1040, Schedule SE, W-2, 941, 943, 944, 940	1065, 941, 943, 940, 1040	1065, 941, 943, 940, 1040	1120, 941, 943, 940	1120S, 941, 943, 940	1065, 941, 943, 940, 1040

*Refer to the IRS website www.irs.gov for the latest and complete filing requirements. In addition, consult a tax professional to ensure correct and accurate filings for your corporate and personal returns.

The United States Small Business Administration (SBA) provides many valuable tools, tips, and free resources on their website www.sba.gov. They offer excellent information on topics, like "Choosing Your Business Structure", "Registering Your Business", "Obtaining Business Licenses", "Learning About Business Law", "Filing & Paying Taxes", and "Business Laws & Regulations." They also provide information about getting local assistance in your area. This website has some very valuable information for small business owners and I would highly recommend spending some time on it.

I OWE HOW MUCH?

My third company was started as an S Corp. We hired an attorney to set up and file the correct paperwork for us. I am so glad we did. It is a several step process for filing the Articles of Incorporation, getting a Federal Tax ID number, filling out the correct IRS forms, and completing the state required forms. In our rush to mail everything back, we left out one IRS form declaring ourselves as an S Corp for tax purposes. We received the approved Articles back and got our tax ID as well. When it came tax time in that first year, we got our return prepared and filed on time. Several months later, we received a letter from the IRS that we owed them $15,680 in penalties for operating as an S Corp without declaring ourselves as one. Remember, S Corps pass all profits or losses on to the shareholder to report on personal tax returns instead of paying taxes on the corporate level. We were shocked at the bill! We thought we had filed all the correct paperwork, and, for a company barely turning a profit in our first year we weren't able to pay this. Thankfully our attorney came to the rescue. He contacted the IRS, provided all the proof of filing, and explained the error. The IRS agreed to waive the penalty in light of his evidence and certified standing with the state. The initial cost of hiring an attorney was well worth it and avoided us having to pay a $15k penalty our first year.

5

SMALL BUSINESS SECRETS

What You Need To Know

At this point, you've got a business model and an actual business. I'm sure you are excited to start selling right away! You're certainly on your way, but still have a few more steps before you are ready to launch the product. I mean, c'mon, we're only a quarter of the way through the book. We still have a lot to discuss. It's important to understand what actually goes into building a successful company. We're going to discuss creating the right culture, building a winning team, managing risk, and overcoming financial challenges. As a small business owner, be prepared to place all this responsibility on your shoulders. Success starts with your actions and you need to be ready for the challenges ahead. This chapter will prepare you to be self-sufficient and build your company the right way. The first 12 months are extremely critical and will be difficult, so starting the right way is vital.

Here's a basic fact of business. You need money to get your product to the market. Unless you are independently wealthy, at some point you'll need to raise capital and find investors. However, as we'll see, taking on investors too soon can have negative results. Starting out you will have to rely on your own resources and capital. This creates a challenge of getting to where you want to be with the limited resources you currently have. This is a common issue every entrepreneur faces. How do I get million dollar results on a thousand-dollar budget? Entrepreneurs must be creative, hard-working, and dedicated in order to get the most out of what they have. You'll be forced to use the capital and resources at your disposal in ways that get the best results. How well you're able to maximize these resources will determine your success. Let's start with the art of Bootstrapping.

BOOTSTRAPPING

Bootstrapping literally means pulling yourself up by your own bootstraps and refers to doing things yourself within your business. As a small business owner starting out, you're going to have limited resources, so you need to make the most of them. You probably won't have much money starting out and it certainly won't be enough to cover all your expenses. The amount of money you make is always related to amount of money you spend. One sure way to fail early is to be careless with your resources. Spending too much money on things right away is a common mistake - renting an expensive office, buying brand new equipment, or hiring a full staff of people to do everything for you.

You want the best. It's a natural urge as a business owner to be the boss and hire people to do the work. You're finally running things and want a certain image for your company. But, as an entrepreneur, you'll have to find ways of doing the job yourself for the least expensive price. This means getting creative, using your network, calling in favors, working hard, and doing whatever it takes to get the job done. That's bootstrapping.

Websites can cost upwards of $10,000 to build. They look very professional, but will cost you a lot of time and money. Instead of hiring an expensive web developer to build your first website, look at purchasing a pre-made template. There are hundreds of quality templates you can buy for under $100 and even some free website templates available online. With a little ingenuity and some time, you can create a functional website for under $200 yourself. Get in the mindset of asking yourself, "Can I accomplish this myself?" You need to find ways of saving money.

Your startup will take time to get off the ground before it starts generating consistent income. Spending less money each month will allow you to turn a profit faster. Most business owner's expectation of when they'll be profitable is wrong. In all honesty, take your timetable and double it. That's more realistic for how long it will take you to see meaningful revenue. You need to plan for sustaining longer on your own. Bootstrapping will allow you to do more with the little money you have. I mentioned earlier: plan to survive for a year. This means you'll have to create marketing and sales yourself.

In addition, there will always be a certain amount of risk involved. During the startup that risk can have more of an impact, because you don't have enough resources to create a buffer or margin for error. Coco-Cola can take a $100,000 hit on redesigning ads, but you can't. Bootstrapping can help limit that risk. Find ways to get the job done cheaply without compromising the quality. You'll be amazed at what can be accomplished for little to no cost. Look at the amount of resources available to you. With a few phone calls and some work that ad redesign may only cost you $1,000, which is more bearable.

Bootstrapping also allows you to operate longer without investors. Your whole purpose of starting a small business is to run your own company. You want to be in charge of the operations and decisions. Having to turn to investors right away puts you at a disadvantage and can really hurt you. Here's an example of what I'm talking about.

When you first start your company, it's not going to be worth much. You don't have much revenue, a large customer base, many assets, or valuable brand power. Your value will most likely be the money you have invested in the physical goods/assets. For this example, let's say your initial value is $50,000 during startup. As your company grows you have more sales, more revenue, more assets, more customers, and greater brand recognition. After two years, your company is now worth $450,000. That's a big difference in value. When you choose to bring in an investor will greatly influence how much of your company that investor gets.

Let's say this investor brings in $50,000 when your company is still young and only worth $50,000. His investment plus your value equal $100,000. Since he brought in $50,000 he receives 50% of your company. However, if you make it to the second year solely on your own resources then his $50,000 investment is a much smaller share. His investment plus your value now equal $500,000. He only receives 10% of your company. Would you rather give up 50% or 10%? This is the power of bootstrapping.

Don't worry about small stuff, like buying the newest computers or coolest office toys. I know you want to pimp out your office and make it look cool. That's a waste of money. Instead, focus your money on things directly related to generating sales - things like the **product, development, customer service, branding,** and building **sales channels**. In your business model, you identified where your customers are and how to reach them. This is where you should be spending your resources. Your goal is to build the business as quickly as possible. Relying on outside capital too soon can be very costly. So the more you can accomplish yourself during the initial growth will payoff down the road. A successful entrepreneur is great at bootstrapping.

ALWAYS ASK

Last year a large convention came to town that I wanted our new product in. However, the product was still in development, so we missed the main registration time. When the product finally was ready there were only four days left before the convention started. I decided to call the convention director anyway and see if they had any open spots we could fill. As it turns out they did have an extra booth but wanted $500 for the booth plus $300 to print flyers and put them in the gift bags. Most of our capital was already tied up in new packaging. Instead I asked if we could donate $500 in product (our cost of goods was $116) to their raffle prizes in exchange for the booth, print our own flyers, and stuff them ourselves. The organizer was excited to get more products to raffle off and agreed. I made a few phone calls and found a local printer that could print 2,000 high quality color rack cards for $130 and have them ready in two days. I then recruited a few friends to help me the day before the convention to sit in the lobby stuffing the gift bags. Instead of paying $800, we were able to get into the convention for $246. We made a few sales, turned a profit, and ended up having a successful weekend. Never be afraid to ask and look for alternative solutions when bootstrapping.

CULTURE

More than likely you will have partners involved in your startup, either with co-founders, bringing on partners, or hiring employees. These are the people you're going to rely on and work closely with. As the business starts to grow, so will the amount of work. Small businesses have the same jobs as a large company, but much fewer people to do them. You'll depend on your partners and employees to take on more responsibility. As an owner, you are going to wear many hats whether you like it or not. Everyone involved with the company will do a little of everything from sales, marketing, design, promotion, and accounting. It's important to select the right people in order to create a successful culture at your company. A strong culture is fundamental for any successful company and can especially affect how well a startup does. A strong culture is also one of the more difficult pieces to predict, create, and control. Every CEO has struggled with it at one time or another. It's now up to you to create that culture, so here are a few tips to help.

Create a moral and responsible culture within your company. In 1991, Warren Buffett took over as interim CEO of Salomon Brothers after their bond scandal. At the time, Salomon faced a barrage of bad publicity, government regulators, and huge possible fines. Buffett identified a poor culture at Salomon ultimately allowing the dishonest practices that led to the company's situation. Buffett knew he had to act quickly in order to turn both the culture and company around. He cancelled many employee perks, changed reward and bonus structures, tightened accountability for actions, and amended stock option plans. He put a large emphasis on upholding ethical and legal standards by challenging his employees to report any misconduct they witnessed directly to him. He even provided in a company-wide memo his personal office number that Salomon employees could call.

Buffett implemented a radical overhaul to set the precedence that immoral action would no longer be tolerated as well as installed a punishment system to hold employees accountable. Buffett also contacted each of Salomon's partners to inform them of the new management and policies. They were open about wrong doings, broken trust, and let partners know they had an obligation to correct their ways. Finally, Buffett took out two-page ads in the Wall Street Journal, New York Post, and The Washington Post, informing shareholders and the public of their new directives for honest business. Buffett spent an enormous amount of time and resources to simply turn the culture around at Salomon Brothers. So why did he go to these great lengths? What purpose did one of the most successful businessmen on the planet have for focusing so much energy on fixing a company's culture?

Warren Buffet knows that a company is only as good as its culture. And when one of the world's largest business mogul sets a precedence, I suggest you take notice. Buffett establishes productive culture in his businesses through leadership. He sets an example of behavior and accountability, and you need to do the same. Culture is a trickle-down environment. A toxic culture will kill your company. Employees learn behavior set by managers above them and will emulate that same culture. As a leader, you must set a good example for employees. Any immoral action on your part demonstrates to employees that they can be dishonest as well. Pay attention to what is going on and how your actions are portrayed. Establish appropriate rewards and consequences for employees, plus always make yourself open to talk with employees. First and foremost, take a lesson from Warren Buffett and establish the right culture at your company.

The second part to building a productive culture is to surround yourself with people who are different from you. It's easy to want like-minded people around you, but that actually holds you back. Instead, look for individuals that are diverse and different from you - people that bring fresh ideas and unique outlooks. Your job as a leader is to build the strongest team possible. You want employees with different skill sets, especially in a small business. You can also help to encourage creativity by mixing up your employees to work on different projects. Experiment with the chemistry of the group and see who works really well together.

As a leader establish clear company goals and execution strategies to reach them, in order to ensure everyone is working towards the same goal. Don't bring in people who are more interested in individual achievements. There needs to be one shared vision of success. But, within that shared goal, find people who work in different ways. The more diversity that you can implement in your company the more ideas you'll generate. In return you'll create a stronger company culture.

Diversity also improves the overall stability of your company. The late Steve Jobs first disclosed that he had pancreatic cancer in 2004. When he announced his resignation from the company in 2009, Apple stock prices dropped over 55%. Public perception of Apple diminished without Jobs at the helm.

On January 20, 2009 Apple stock dropped to $78.20 per share, while just six months earlier Apple had traded for $176 per share. Could one person really have that great of an effect? As the owner of your company, you like to feel that you're irreplaceable. You want to have control over decisions and gain a sense of accomplishment from your actions. In reality, however, it may hurt your company. If all the creativity and success is derived from one person, then an enormous amount is lost if anything ever happens to that person.

Investors also look for well-rounded management teams. They want to see your company has industry experience, market knowledge, and proven success with similar products. Investors tend to have more confidence in a complete team than in just one person. When you approach investors for capital, expect them to analyze the depth of your co-founders and advisors. Investors may see more value with a diverse team supporting you, and could deny funding if they feel you're lacking necessary experience or depth.

Your mission is placing people in the best position to succeed. When you start to hire people around you, it's better to have a complete team making decisions together - a team you can rely on to get things done. In the event a person leaves, the company is better situated if others are capable of stepping in. Plus, a more diverse team is able to reach higher. Be aware of the risks you create within your company, in the eyes of the investors, and especially for any shareholders. While you may want to be the final decision maker, having a complimentary executive team may be the best thing for your company.

THE RUBBERBAND BALL

The example that I give people about culture is to envision a giant rubber band ball. They are made up of all sorts of rubber bands. The rubber bands are different sizes and different colors. They are set at all different angles and layers around the ball. Some rubber bands are close to the middle, while others are on the outside. There is not one rubber band on there that's exactly like another. And, man, do those things bounce high. A company should not be like salmon spawning in a river, where every fish is a like and pointing in the same direction upstream. Dynamic companies are like rubber band balls with different employees at various angles all circling around the same central goal. All their ideas and production overlap each other to form a solid structure and together you can bounce really high.

Finally, try not to go into business with your friends. Many relationships have been hurt or completely ruined by a business. While it may seem like a fun idea to running a company with your friends, remember that it is a business. Often times, when difficult decisions need to be made, friendships get in the way of smart choices. You'll make concessions to your friends in situations that you normally wouldn't. Authority is more difficult to establish between friends than it is with normal manager/employee relationships. I have personally lost three close friends over starting a business with them. These were close friends I thought would be great to work with every day. Now we don't speak at all. One of them I was dating at the time and stress from the business spilled over into our relationship. We were 50/50 partners in my real estate development company. Decisions about the direction of the company, expenses, and finance problems wore on the relationship for two years and eventually contributed to our break up. I feel like almost every entrepreneur I talk with says the same thing-"Starting this business almost led to my divorce." Try to leave out personal relationships when you bring on partners. It really impacts the quality of your business decisions and effectiveness as a leader. If you're not able to treat your friend like an employee and get results from them, then don't risk it. Save yourself the difficulty down the road and handle this startup as a business from the beginning.

RISK

To this point, we haven't talked a lot about risk. You've examined the market place, know who your competitors are, understand various market forces, and are trying to predict consumer buying patterns. This is all great information for understanding market risks, but let's take a moment to be honest about the other risks involved. There are a variety of risks with starting and running a small business. Many states required business owners to purchase liability insurance to protect companies. Let's examine some of the other risks you need to be aware of as you move forward.

BARRIERS TO ENTRY

Are you starting a software company with a new type of operating system and plan to compete with Microsoft Windows? That's about as big of a barrier to entry I can think of - high research and development costs, high operating and manufacturing costs, established sales channels, expensive marketing, few substitute products, and one very large competitor. Barriers to entry are the challenges that stand in your way of introducing your product to the market. Certain markets have low barriers to entry and others have very high barriers to entry. Starting a landscape company has very low barriers to entry - buying a few hundred dollars of equipment, gas money, and basic marketing costs. Owning an NFL team has very high barriers to entry - extremely expensive, dependent on voting and approvals, costly marketing, and requirement of key partnerships.

A market with low barriers to entry means it is easy for you to get started, but it also means it's easy for others to get started in also. There are likely to be many competitors and substitute products. This may impact your ability to charge a premium price or your ability to differentiate. High barriers of entry make it extremely difficult to get started, but, once you're established and on the other side of the barrier, it's likely you'll have fewer competitors. This can make it easier to gain market share (consumers simply don't have many options to choose from) and determine your own pricing. Make sure to identify what barriers exist, what it'll take to get over them, and what they mean for your revenue.

LEGAL LIABILITY

It is easy to be excited about your own product, but consumers or outside groups may not share the sentiment. Lawsuits are very common and can be incredibly costly or damaging. It is important to consider possible legal liabilities you may run into. Examine your product and make a list of potential risks it can cause. Make sure to protect yourself against those risks. Label warnings and clear instructions are one of your best defenses. You see warnings on almost every product sold today. Even coffee cups have warnings on them to not spill the hot beverage on you. Don't assume that something is intuitive for the consumer. Invest in having any necessary laboratory testing done and verified by reputable labs. Have the results showing your product was tested safe, in case any lawsuits do arise. If you find that your product is not 100% safe, then it's worthwhile to delay any product launch in order to fix the problem. Take some time now to avoid any potential legal liabilities you may run into.

TIMING

You may not initially think of timing as a risk, but market conditions and consumer readiness are absolutely risks. These two factors will dictate if there is a demand for your product. Market conditions need to be right for consumers to feel confident buying your product. During our last recession in the US markets, new home sales plummeted. Many real estate agents and developers went out of business. The market was not optimal for buying new homes. You wouldn't start a new real estate development company, and invest thousands of dollars, while the housing market was collapsing. From your Market Analysis in Chapter 1, you know what the current political, technological, consumer, and economic conditions are. That analysis shows you the strength of each market force and how it will impact you. That is why it's a good idea to perform a Market Analysis annually to track any changing conditions.

Consumers must also be ready to accept your product. Products featuring a new technology are a great example of this. You'll have a few early adapters willing to try your product, but the mass population is much slower to adapt to something new. You can have a great product, but you won't make any sales unless the consumer sees a need for it in their life. New technologies are often not widely adapted, until they have spent some time on the market and customers have time to adapt to it. Be careful introducing something completely new to the market when there's nothing else like it. You'll have to do much more marketing and consumer education than if your product is something the consumer already has an understanding of.

AHEAD OF ITS TIME

Can you name what the first smartphone was? No, it wasn't an Apple iPhone, Samsung, or Nokia. In 1992, IBM and Bellsouth introduced the Simon Personal Communicator. The Simon was a cellphone that had email, mobile apps, a touch screen display, virtual keyboard, and even sent faxes. The first iPhone wasn't introduced until June 29, 2007, over 15 years after the Simon. So why have you not heard of the Simon? Simply put, it was ahead of its time. Consumers were just getting used to the thought of a mobile phone and weren't ready to accept the Simon's technology. They hadn't adapted to the possibility of having email on their phone. Now, we can't imagine going without it, but that process took a decade. Plus, the Simon was large, heavy, and expensive. The technology hadn't progressed far enough to make it easy for consumers to adopt. Technology needed more time to develop a more user-friendly smartphone. Simply introducing the latest technology or product first doesn't guarantee success. Consumers have to be ready to accept your product.

FINANCIAL

Entrepreneurs are gamblers. They are putting their money on the table and rolling the dice to see if this company will pay off. Starting your business will require upfront capital and most of that will come from you. Few startups receive SBA loans or investors, until they actually have some sales. Plus, as we mentioned before, you may not want to take on investors early in the game until you have some time to build the value of your company. Getting it off the ground will be up to you and it will require some of your own money to do this. Paying for attorney costs, websites, packaging, branding, and marketing out of your own pocket can get expensive. Remember, don't bet what you can't afford to lose.

The second company I started was a cosmetic product - a new wrinkle treatment made from natural and active ingredients. My partners and I were incredibly excited over this and knew it would be successful. The only problem was that it required a large amount of capital up front to buy the rights, purchase inventory, design packaging, print labels, branding, and advertising. We were just out of grad school, so none of us had much money, but we didn't want to let this opportunity pass us by. So I took a chance and invested my entire savings of $36,000.

I guarantee you'll find yourself in a similar situation. All entrepreneurs believe their product is a gold mine and want to see it succeed. There will come a time when you'll have to put your money in. Most likely, that time will come over and over again and you'll keep investing your own money. You will have to decide how much financial risk you can afford to take. Like gambling, do not put in more than you can lose.

Investing my life savings was a big risk. The business did not take off immediately and I did not receive a single payout the first year. However, I planned for that and still had consistent income coming in each month. I made sure my mortgage was paid for each month and I could still buy groceries. Several years later, I still have not recouped that investment personally. So, do not invest more than you can afford to be without. There is no set timeline on collecting an income or getting your investment out when running a small business.

BE PROFESSIONAL

With the explosion of smartphones, texting, and social media, we often forget what professional communication is. Abbreviations and pop culture slang have become normal in our society. They have crept into mainstream business every day. With instant messages and social media, we're losing the knowledge how to communicate professionally.

My friend forwarded me this email yesterday that she received from a cosmetics sales rep. It shocked me this was the rep's idea of professional communication. I was so surprised by it, that I had to include it in this book for you to see. I've excluded the company name to protect their reputation, but this is her exact email word-for-word. She actually sent this to her contacts and potential customers:

> *OMGosh..*
>
> *Ladies n Gents:) some exciting news.. I'm officially 400$*
> *from DIQ (director in qualification) and being on target*
> *my car in XXXX XXX!! I'm selling mascara n an eye*
> *makeup remover for 30$.. By purchasing that, u will*
> *recieve an eye shadow or eyeliner of ur choice as a*
> *gift:)!!! This is a great gift for someone special, or of*
> *course just for yourself! Can u help me reach my goals??*
> *Text me back or go onto www.xxxxxxx.come/tracilee to*
> *place an order! Thank you so much!*

How professional does this email look? How many grammatical and spelling errors do you see? She explains her motivation, but where is the benefit to the consumer? Even her contact email link is misspelled, directing any client to a broken webpage. Based on this email, would you purchase cosmetics from her?

Any communication you have with people, whether it's an advertisement, email, website, text, order confirmation, online chat, in person, or phone call, needs to be professional. How well you communicate, directly reflects upon your business and image. Always use proper grammar. If your high school English teacher would not approve of what you have written, then you may want to revise it. Bad communication skills, like the email above, will reflect very poorly on your business. Make certain your call to action is clear and that your contact information is correct. You will lose any potential customers that you have worked hard to get. You may only have one chance to get in front of a potential customer. What you say and how you say it, will determine if they buy from you. Once that customer is gone, you've lost them. When you design your marketing campaign, continually remind yourself that this may be your only chance to communicate with your customer. What do you want to say with that one shot?

In addition, always practice professional behavior whenever you are in a business setting. Again, you are representing your company and it reflects upon your image. How well you present yourself, will determine the tone of the meeting or interaction. I continually witness people forgetting the basics of professionalism. So much so, that people with good skills, really stand out. Here are a few of the basics:

- **Dress professionally**
- **Make good eye-contact**
- **Smile (even when talking on the phone)**
- **Firm handshake**
- **Remember names**
- **Be polite**
- **Strong and engaging tone of voice**
- **No swearing**
- **Be social and interact with others**
- **Stay positive**
- **Don't put others down**

- **Don't dominate the conversation**

Spend time to improve your professionalism and communication skills. Ask your friends and co-workers to evaluate your level of professionalism. Get their feedback on how well you are doing. If you are uncomfortable with any of these topics or need to improve in any areas, there are plenty of great resources available. Search online for tips and hints to improve your skills. One book I highly recommend is *Crucial Conversations, Tools for talking when stakes are high* by Kerry Patterson. The techniques presented are incredibly useful for any business owner. The knowledge you gain just may be the difference, between earning a customer and wasting an opportunity.

Personally, I hope to never see an email like that one again. As you move forward with your business, you must understand the importance of professional communication. There is so much at stake, with every interaction. How you handle it and how well you present yourself, will ultimately determine your success.

BE HONEST

Finally, be honest with yourself when it comes to your business. Entrepreneurs have high aspirations and goals. That's what makes us dreamers and visionaries. Sometimes those visions can cloud reality, causing you to fall short. It's a common mistake to over-estimate revenue projections or timelines when you're first getting started. For my second business, my partners and I created what we thought was an accurate financial plan. We took weeks carefully examining all the market factors and customer buying trends. The plan had three columns for low, conservative, and high revenue projections. Our lowest projection forecasted making $430,000 in revenue and turning a $200,000 profit in our first year. Then reality set in. The product took longer to get to market, it was harder to differentiate than we thought, customers didn't instantly accept it, more marketing costs were required and shipping costs increased. In actuality, we only made a total of $35,000 in revenue and posted a $36,000 loss. The second year more closely resembled our plan, so our timeline ended up taking twice as long and the first year revenue was only 12% of our projections. I still look at that plan periodically as a reminder that the best made forecasts can fall short. Be honest when it comes to setting goals and projections.

- When will the product be ready for market?
- What are the real operation costs?
- How much money do we have?
- What will our sales conversion rate be?
- How dynamic are we?
- Who are our competitors?
- How many liabilities do we have?

You are going to run into questions like this on a daily basis. Be realistic when answering them and it will set you up to succeed.

6

GREAT BRANDING

Create What Everyone Wants

T his is one of the biggest challenges you'll face. Branding is lightning in a bottle. You're not sure what it is and it is hard as hell to capture. It's not something you can buy or predict. Branding is a goal you work towards-a canvas you try to paint for your customer. Branding is one of the most important topics to focus on while building your business. Everyone has a 7-step, 10-step, or 12-step list for successful branding. We're going to ignore those. That's because there isn't a set blueprint for branding. You can give me a 12-step plan to paint a masterpiece, but that doesn't mean I can do it. Instead of a step plan, let's focus on what goes into branding and help you understand the layers that create it. In this chapter, we'll discuss in detail exactly what good branding is. Just maybe you'll be able to capture a little of that lightning in a bottle.

™

This is one of the best examples of good branding. What do you think of when you see this image? I don't need to explain anything and you already know this is Nike. With a single glance you know who the company is, what they do, and what their tagline is. Same thing if you hear the tagline or the company name. It's not complicated or something you need to think about. Nike kept it very simple when they created their patented symbol and tagline. You can associate the company name, image, or logo with exactly what they do-same thing with McDonalds, Target, or Audi.

Branding is created from your company's values and culture, and reflects your understanding of the customer's needs. It is a way for your customers to connect with you and find your products. It's your company name, the look and feel of your logo, your tagline, your identity, and your image. Most importantly, it is your customer's perception of you. Branding is measured on how well a customer understands you from a simple logo or tagline. Branding gives your company meaning and quickly communicates that message to the customer. It is your company's personality. You have to develop a brand strategy before you spend anything on marketing or advertising. Building your brand is critical. Without branding, your company doesn't have an identity.

Let's play a quick word game to illustrate this point. Write down the first word that comes to your mind.

COMPANY	IMAGE OR PERCEPTION
VOLVO	
DISNEY	
FORD	
ORBITZ	

See how quickly you associated a description to these companies? You have a perception of them based on the brand they've built. Now, let's determine what your branding will be about. You already know what makes you unique and your position in the market. Brainstorm for a bit and answer each of these questions about your company. This will help identify other qualities about your company.

BRANDING ANALYSIS

BRAND AWARENESS	BRAND IDENTITY	BRAND IMAGE
Does the company name have meaning?	What symbols represent your meaning?	What image lends credibility?
What tagline would support that meaning?	What colors represent you and your product?	What image influences the customer's experience?
What are your values?	What demonstrates your core values?	What image helps differentiate our product?
What are your personality traits?	What style represents your personality?	What image demonstrates our principles?
What is your background or story?	What message do you want to convey to customers?	What image resonates with the customer?
What is your promise to the customer?	What does this company want to be known for?	

These answers help determine what images and sayings you present to customers. This information will shape their perception of you. Now that you've got some these on paper, let's break down the individual components of building a brand.

- **CREATION** – Start by defining who you are and what your brand is. Look at your answers above and create a brand message. Be genuine about your goals and personality. Create a brand from your core mission, vision, values, goals, personality, and position.

- **LOGOS**– Logos add a visual element and style to your brand. A logo should be simple, have a clean looking style, and be eye catching. Sketch out some images that personify your company or product. Ask friends for input on which ones they like the best. Experiment with colors, fonts, and shapes to find the best looking combination. Be bold to make the image or name stand out on packaging and advertising. Logos don't need to be complicated. Good logos are simple, unique, and memorable. They reflect your company's values and objectives. Research several brands that you like or stand out to you, and look at what elements they've incorporated.

- **SYMBOLS & IMAGERY** – Our culture is full of symbols that already have established meaning. Instead of trying to create new symbols, try incorporating existing ones. Customers are already familiar with many symbol meanings. If your message is captured through a cultural symbol, then look at using it appropriately in your branding.

- **FONTS** – Each font provides a different image and personality. Picking the right font can add meaning to your product. Experiment with different fonts to find the right one that embodies your style. Make sure to consider legibility and clearness. Can your customer recognize it from far away?

- **COLORS** – picking the right colors is important as well. Use colors that your customers identify with and create the right feeling for your product. If you are an organic food company, blues, greens, and earth tones give a more natural feel. Ferrari uses yellow, red, and black to convey boldness in their style. Just like mood rings, color can quickly portray your image and attitude.

- **PERSONALIZATION** – Often customers identify quickly with personalized logos or branding-names like Steve's Pizza or Hometown Sporting Goods versus generic names. Consumers connect with a more personal message. Think about ways to tell your story to customers. Let them know who you are and where your product comes from. Find ways to connect with your customers.

- **TRENDS** – Many businesses look to capitalize on current trends. It may be appealing to create a logo or tagline based on trend. However, remember trends are just that.

They will end shortly. Think of a catch phrase from a one hit wonder five years ago. Do you still like it?

- **EVOLVE** – Create a brand that can evolve with the times. Design a logo that colors or layout can be updated and still retain the core elements. Think of something that can be dynamic and cross over time periods. Your market place and customers will change over time. Measure the effectiveness of your message by your return on investment. Monitor your feedback and analytics. If people aren't searching for you or clicking on your site, then your brand isn't resonating well. Adapt to the current market place to better connect with your customers.

- **PROMISE** – Think of the questions above concerning what promises you are making to the customer? Does your name or logo reflect that? Create an image that communicates your values and promise to the customer. This is also a great way to personalize your brand. Demonstrate what the customer will receive from your product. That can be quality, price, a unique experience, or any number of benefits. Communicating your promise will help create confidence with the customer.

- **VALUE** – Clearly communicate the benefit your product delivers. Branding connects your value proposition with the customer. Don't get caught up talking about the technology or manufacturing process. Keep the message focused on the value and benefits. What is the customer going to get out of this? The market is full of competitors looking to out-do each other. Elevate your brand to offer customers something more and create a superior value proposition. This will help you stand out to the customer. Let your value do the talking.

- **TAGLINE** – A few catchy words that describe your style or message, taglines reflect your product promises and utilize a key phrase. Those key phrases can be verbal actions, descriptions, positions, or questions. Consumers understand what you do just by hearing it. And you don't have to stick with the same tagline forever. Feel free to change it periodically as your company evolves. Just make sure it captures your message. Below are a few taglines to demonstrate this point:

COMPANY	TAGLINE
COMMANDS ACTION	
YouTube	Broadcast Yourself
MINI Cooper	Let's Motor

| Microsoft | Be What's Next |
| Apple | Think Different |

DESCRIBES THE SERVICE

Target	Expect More, Pay Less
MSNBC	The Whole Picture
Allstate	You're In Good Hands
GE	Imagination At Work

POSITION STATEMENT

BMW	The Ultimate Driving Machine
British Airways	The Way To Fly
National Guard	Americans At Their Best

THOUGHT PROVOKING

Sears	Where Else?
Metropolitan Life Insurance	Have You Met Life Today?
Dairy Council	Got Milk?

SPECIFIC CATEGORY

AT&T	The World's Networking Company
HSBC	The World's Bank
NYSE	The World Puts Its Stock In Us

- **PROVOKE EMOTION** – Buying is an emotional experience for customers. Most often, because they're excited about the benefits, it makes them feel good, they are improving their life, or they got a great deal and are saving money. Sales are driven by emotions. In your branding, create an emotion for people-something that motivates them and makes them want to try your product. Good branding connects with people emotionally and makes your product desirable.

- **BE DISRUPTIVE** – Consumers already have products they like that fit their needs. When introducing a new product, you need to be disruptive to their current way of doing things. Get them to think about the benefits differently, look at the products in a new way, make them want more out of their products, and change their buying patterns. Change the consumer's preferences to favor your product. Your branding should yell, "Hey don't pick up your normal stuff...buy my new product instead! Your life will be better for it!"

- **CREATE A CULTURE** – Brands can extend beyond a name or logo. The better brands create an entire culture or a lifestyle around them. Simply look at Harley-Davidson motorcycles and the culture they have created. 'Harley' owners are staunchly loyal, extremely passionate about their bikes, differentiate themselves as Harley riders, and connect with other people who also own Harley Davidsons. The company has done such a great job with branding, that their products have become a lifestyle. Look at how you can create a culture around your product with events, clothing, style, or image. Consumers love to connect with each other and be part of a culture. Develop ways your customers can be part of something bigger by owning your product. Make it easy for them to share the experience. Think about exclusive clubs, reward programs, special events, social media, and forums. Look at companies, like Harley Davidson, Red Bull, and Ford, and how they developed their brand into a culture.

- **NURTURE** – Once you start to make sales and build a culture, don't stop there. Continue to reach out to customers and reward them! This is where Content Marketing and building automated sales funnels becomes so vital. Consumers spend their time and money to help your business grow, so continue to build that relationship. Nurturing loyalty will result in more return customers and higher revenue. After all, keeping an existing customer is much cheaper than earning a new one, and existing customers are much easier to sell to. The result? Higher margins! Keep that in mind when developing your rewards. Recognition doesn't need to be costly or elaborate. A simple thank you letter or personal recognition is plenty. Continue engaging them with great content marketing campaigns. Ask them to write a review or make a quick post featured on your website. It's a win-win. Find ways to connect further with your customers long after the sale. Reward them for their loyalty.

- **STRATEGY** – Consumers are blasted with hundreds of advertisements every day. Most of them we don't even pay attention to and are used to blocking out. Develop a content strategy to make your message count. Refer back to the Business Model and Integrated Marketing strategies we talked about in chapter 2. You know where your customers are and how to reach them. Build your brand with a strategy that relates to those customers. Your business model, sales plan, and marketing plan must all be in line with each other. They are your company's infrastructure. Branding ties them all together. In business, don't do things randomly, hoping to see results. This is called *Hope Marketing*, and it doesn't work. Develop a strategy that fits specific objectives and maximize your efforts.

- **MEASUREMENT** – finally pay attention to your results. Monitor what type of return and response you are getting. Do you have a high bounce rate on your website or low feedback on your posts? We've talked about all the tools available - from analytics to surveys and forums. Keep a close watch on how well your message is resonating with customers and how they are reacting to it. Interpret the things you are and aren't seeing. You may think you've got a great strategy, but customers don't have to agree with you. Paying customers ultimately decide how successful your branding is. If you aren't connecting well with people, your revenue will suffer. Monitor analytics on a daily basis and find ways to improve. Be consistent with your message. There are hundreds of ways you can communicate that message. Use the resources available to you to tweak the marketing campaign into a finely tuned machine.

- **TRADEMARKS & PATENTS** – As you are creating your brand, make sure to research existing trademarks and avoid any infringement. Maybe that logo idea in your head is actually a trademarked logo you saw a few years ago. It is important to fully research your ideas before actually launching them. A trademark can include words, names, images or symbols to distinguish a brand. You don't want to copy any trademarks or protected property inadvertently. Visit the US Patent and Trademark online search at www.uspto.gov. There you can search names, logos, patents, and get lots of valuable information about filing your own trademarks. The government has done a great job of creating an easy to navigate site with free information and news. Take time to perform your due diligence before launching any brand names, taglines, or logos.

I often get asked if business owners should file their own trademarks and patents. The question I usually ask them is, "Does your brand identity depend on it? If another company picked a similar logo or name, does it significantly detract from your brand?" Examine your market and competitors to determine if you need to take action protecting your branding. If the answer is "yes", then I would recommend trademarking your brand (name, logo, tagline). There are plenty of trademark filing services or trademark attorneys available; however, the US Patent and Trademark online site makes it pretty easy to do yourself. They have a step by step guide for first time filers. Visit their pages www.uspto.gov/trademarks/basics and www.uspto.gov/inventors/trademarks.jsp to start your process. The cost can range from $275-$325 per filing class and could be well worth the cost to protect your property.

Filing for a patent is different than a trademark. The patent process is more complicated and costly. A patent can take up to several years and cost upwards of $10,000. If you consider filing for a patent, I recommend you consult with a patent attorney first. Their upfront cost can save you thousands of dollars and provide valuable advice. Patents are meant to protect a process, machine, composition, innovations, or improvements on existing products. They can be useful for a something very unique or revolutionary. However, very few products actually require a patent. I have not elected to patent any of my products to date. The process is expensive and patents can be circumvented, if competitors change at least one significant detail. Just look at brand versus generic drugs at your local pharmacy or grocery store. Drug companies spend millions of dollars on patents, yet there is a generic brand for almost every drug or medicine on the market. So, for all the time, effort, and expense you put towards a patent, it could be useless if a competitor changes one detail on their product. I personally don't feel that patents offer you absolute protection nor are worthwhile during the startup phase. You can use that money better elsewhere. Carefully weigh the pros and cons of filing for a patent, consult with a patent attorney, and determine if it is absolutely necessary before starting this process.

Branding is a process that takes daily work without any promise of return. It is a challenge based on consumer reactions and changing forces. Don't get frustrated, if you don't see results right away. There are no exact answers or absolute formulas to do this. The ideas presented are a foundation for building your brand, but are certainly not the only ideas you can use. There may be other unique ways to create a brand based on your product or market. Branding is a combination of many layers. No one single item completely makes up a brand. You have to integrate many different ideas and influences. A strong brand leads to better customer perceptions, higher brand recognition, and how much the customer is willing to pay for your product. A complete brand retains more existing customers and offers them an experience. Branding is what separates the successful companies from the unknowns.

If you are not getting the results you want from building your own brand, there are professionals out there that will do it for you. Branding professionals specialize in creating brands and can provide you valuable information, not to mention have all the tools required to build all the layers of your brand. They will interview you about all the questions you answered above about your company, values, mission, and message. They'll create logos, packaging, websites, marketing, advertising, and anything else you need. They'll also run focus groups and product testing to get actual consumer feedback. They can be very useful to get you started on the right track. A branding expert will design a professional-looking campaign to help your company look bigger and more established right from the start.

The downside is that they can be costly. We used a branding professional to help create our brand and it cost us over $13,000 up front. The results were great and I felt so much better about having a professional on board, but it didn't leave us much money for advertising. One reason it took our company longer than expected to start making revenue was because we had to scale back our advertising plan. We had a great looking product, but couldn't advertise it the way we needed. We had to get more capital before launching our full marketing campaign. As a small business, you are going to have to decide where and when to spend money.

Hindsight is 20/20, so here's my solution to this dilemma. Your brand matters so hire a professional. Do as much of the legwork for branding as you can. Answer the questions above, create a strategy, know the overall vision of the brand you want, and put together a complete package. Understand exactly how you are going to structure it. Then hire a branding professional to put the finishing touches on it. This will limit the total cost, while still getting the same professional result. Plus, a quality firm will get the job done on time and help get your product launched sooner. It will benefit you to have a branding specialist on board during the startup phase. Work out a budget that's no more than 20% of your startup capital. Anything over that will limit you in other areas. Hiring a branding professional is a smart decision that will save you time and produce the results you want.

Finding the right company is important and can make a big difference. There are many firms out there that claim to be the best. To find a good branding company do some research on who comes recommended. It is unlikely larger firms will take startups for a low price. Many large branding/marketing firms have a $250,000 minimum budget, but that doesn't mean they don't want to help you. Smart marketing firms realize that small companies today are the large companies tomorrow. Contact some large firms in your area, explain that you are a startup in search of a good branding professional, and ask them whom they recommend.   Make a list to evaluate those companies on how well they communicate their own value and portfolio. Most marketing firms will list past projects and clients on their site. Contact the firms that impress you and start from there.

There you go. That's branding 101. Branding will be one of the most challenging goals you face and will be a daily activity. Remember, it reflects your personality, so have fun with it. Branding represents you. Good luck creating yours.

7

SIMPLE SALES PLANS

Your Guide To Success

Now it's time to write your one-year sales plan. A well-written sales plan is key to meeting your goals and will keep you on track throughout the year. It contains all the information we've been discussing so far with one significant addition – financials. You're going to set a financial goal and this sales plan will be your road map to achieving it. It will break down all the information you have gathered so far into smaller manageable steps and timelines. This sales plan is also used when pitching to investors and applying for SBA loans. They want to know financial projections and potential growth in the market. This plan will detail exactly what they are looking for.

By now, you're an expert on your customers, their buying patterns, and the market. That's good, because we're about to get a lot more detailed. We're going to take that 30,000' view and drop down to the ground level. This sales plan will put actual numbers to your projections. You'll create lists of specific actions to make your strategy a reality. It's time to start thinking about your business in terms of revenue.

For each of these topics, write a paragraph describing it in terms of numbers and values. You've already done the overview back in Chapter 1. Now let's assign real values to these.

1. **THE VALUE OF YOUR PRODUCT** – What are the unique attributes of your product and how much is that worth to the customer? I previously gave the example of a new fuel additive that saves the average driver $50/month in gas. The price of the additive is $40, because it still saves the customer $10/month. Perhaps your product offers a time savings, peace of mind or intangible value instead. How much value does your product add and can you directly charge that amount? Detail what your product does and how much a customer would be willing to pay for that benefit.

2. **POSITION IN THE MARKET** – What niche do you fill and who are your customers? More importantly, how willing and able are they to afford your product? Take the information about your customer's age, location, and economic conditions, and relate it to their buying power/ability. Are your customers price-sensitive and are you introducing a higher priced product? Are they more quality driven and are you selling a lower priced option?

Detail out the spending power and price sensitivity your customers have. Look at current economic conditions and pricing factors in the market. How does it relate to selling your product?

3. **PRICING STRATEGY** - Determine where you fit in the market as it relates to pricing. I hate to bring trigonometry into this, but a simple graph will help illustrate this point well. Draw a graph with the y-axis as price and the x-axis as quality. Place your competitors where they fit for their quality and how much they charge. On the example below, I used different sized diamonds to represent the size of the competitor. Now, place yourself on the graph as the square. This will give you an idea of what your position is and your possible price range. Is there where you want to be? If not, you may need to adjust your pricing strategy.

Price

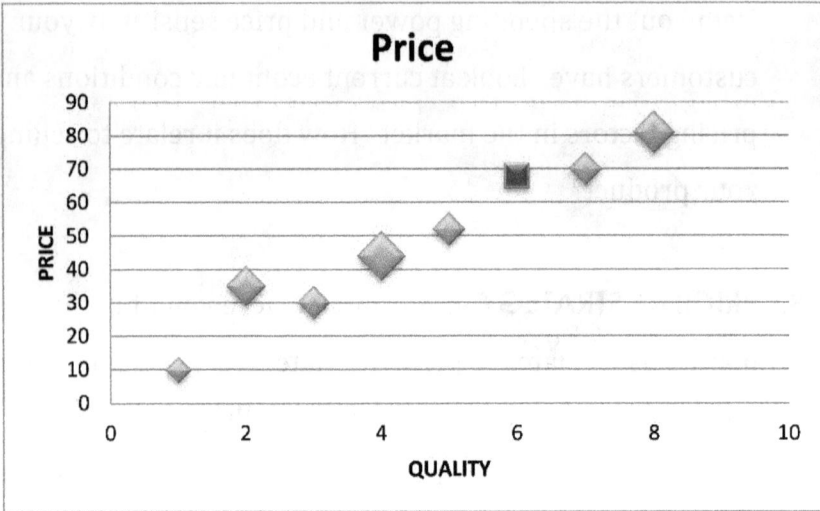

4. **REVENUE GOALS** – There are two ways to forecast your annual revenue. The first is by a straight line approach. Write down your revenue goal and divide it by 12. This is your monthly revenue goal consistently spread over every month. The second method includes market forces and accounts for changing revenue. For example, if you sell snow blowers, your revenue is not going to be consistent every month of the year. You will have a few peak months of sales and then it will taper off. Set your year-end revenue goal, pick a method, and work backwards to come up with monthly revenue numbers. Be as realistic and honest as possible. Account for product development time, barriers to entry, testing, marketing, shipping, consumer buying trends, seasonal factors, and economic conditions. If the numbers aren't adding up, then you need to adjust

your year-end figure. This gives you a guide of monthly revenue required to meet your goal.

5. **SALES CHANNELS** – Detail each of the channels you are going to sell in, how much they will cost, overhead involved, and expected revenue. Try to cover everything you can think of, although don't kill yourself calculating every penny. You just listed your year-end revenue goal, so each of these sales channels should add up to that figure. List out if you'll sell through store fronts, online, partnerships, or however else you plan to reach your customers. List basic income and expenses for each sales channel. Total them all up, then calculate a percentage that each channel represents. This will show you where your highest revenue is projected so you can focus on those areas. It will also predict where to expect the highest margins from. Remember, during the startup phase, lower costs relate to higher revenue.

6. **ADVERTISING** – Next you will forecast your advertising costs for each of the sales channels you have just listed. You are probably thinking how glad you are buying this book, since everything is laid out linearly and easy to follow. List how you plan to reach your customers in each of the sales channels and how much that will cost every month. For example, your online website could include

hosting fees, developer costs, merchant service fees, banner ads, Google Ad Words, sponsored links, social media ads and paid promotions. Focus on your higher margin sales channels, since those will maximize your revenue at the beginning. Evaluate the cost-versus-return for each advertising plan. Project which plan could result in the greatest revenue and list them in ascending order.

7. **MARKETING** – There is an important distinction between advertising and marketing. They are different actions and should not be interchanged as the same thing. Marketing includes advertising, but represents so much more. We'll get into this further when we talk about writing your marketing plan. For now, list out the marketing actions for each sales channel. This may include email marketing, content marketing, trade shows, partnerships, direct mail, online and phone sales, or affiliate programs. One marketing idea can cover several sales channels, but try to detail them out. Describe how you are going to reach potential customers and how much it will cost.

8. **INTANGIBLES** – I rarely include this when describing sales plans, but it's worth mentioning. If your product has opportunities for additional revenue, list it here: revenue that falls outside the normal sales channels, such as **government grants, dividends,** or **tax breaks**; items that

will help your financial bottom line outside the normal revenue streams. Investors will not put much emphasis on this category, but it is important to note any additional factors that can financially help you.

You've just created a one-year financial projection and detailed the steps of how you're going to get there. Your sales plan doesn't need to be complicated, but it should be detailed. This is your financial snap shot to use throughout the year. As market conditions change, update the plan as needed. Keeping your sales plan current will keep you on track to hit your goal every year. It can take a lot of the surprises and unknowns out of the process by detailing each step. You'll be able to see which sales channels have the most revenue potential and the ones worth investing more in. You'll also be able to talk intelligently with investors about your projected revenue and back it up with this sales plan. Many small business owners starting out don't have a detailed sales plan and this will help you stand out to potential investors.

DON'T YOU DARE

Don't rely on social media as a sales tool. If you wrote anywhere in your sales plan that you're going to monetize from social media, cross it out. Social media is a great marketing engine used to engage customers, communicate, and drive traffic. Just because you use Facebook, Twitter or Instagram doesn't guarantee sales. If you planned on social media to be another commerce channel, then I'm sorry to say you'll be disappointed. Social media is a personal way to connect with customers and get your message out. Use it to start conversations, post interesting content and direct people to your product. It is not a sales tool. We will get much more into successful social media strategies in chapter 12.

8

POWERFUL MARKETING PLANS

From Strategy To Reality

How confident are you feeling now compared to when you started this journey? Do the barriers seem as high? Relax. If you've put in the effort to go through each of these chapters, then you're ahead of most people in the same situation. You can make smart decisions about launching your product and avoid a lot of the common mistakes. You can be confident moving forward that you are making good choices.

It's time to write your Marketing Plan. A Marketing Plan is a detailed, well-written projection of your marketing strategy and actions. It details what steps you are going to take to reach your customers. It will help you form specific strategies for startup and entering into your markets. I'll outline some easy steps for writing a detailed marketing plan. This will give you a clear picture of what actions you are going to take in order to launch your product.

Everything you've done leading up to this point will go into the Marketing Plan. We're going to put it all together in a clear plan of action. Again, we're going to keep this simple. A marketing plan doesn't need to be complicated or lengthy; it just needs to be detailed. It should be understandable to people both inside and outside of your company. As you write this out, try to keep it under 10 pages. Any longer and your message will get lost in all the information. There are lots of ways to write a Marketing Plan, so, we'll strip this down to the basics, get rid of the fluff and focus on the important points.

BE SMARTER

S.M.A.R.T.E.R. Goals are a way of writing your projections and end goals. S.M.A.R.T.E.R. stands for **S**pecific, **M**easurable, **A**ttainable, **R**elevant, **T**imed, **E**ffective and **R**ewards. This is a simple way of thinking about your plan. Whatever strategy you create should meet each of these criteria. If you want better customer service, come up with a realistic plan that has clear actions, can actually be achieved with your resources, and has a due date. Make sure that your strategy is understandable, achievable, effective and has rewards at the end. Be S.M.A.R.T.E.R. with your plan and you'll see better results.

---

1. **INTRODUCTION** - Write a brief overview about your product, the problem it solves, the value it adds, and the current market conditions. Why are you starting this company and what do you hope to accomplish? What are your overall objectives and goals? This provides readers with background information and familiarizes them with

your approach. The introduction should include the purpose of your plan and contain enough information to lay the foundation for the rest of your blueprint.

2. **DASHBOARD** - The dashboard is a quick visual of your goals based on a timeline. It can be a chart, graph, or picture-something that gives the reader a simple understanding of what you're working for, measurable milestones, and the timeline you're working within. The Financial Projection from your Sales Plan that you just created is a great dashboard image to include. You can either keep it by month or switch it by quarter for one year. This gives the reader a specific snapshot of your desired results.

3. **TARGET MARKET** - Describe your target market in detail from the research you've done. I've provided a general outline of important points you'll want to include. For each of these you should include a paragraph on your objectives and then go into your strategy. That provides a nice overview and consistent format for the reader to follow.

Objectives

- **Market share** – What is the total size of the market you're going after? How many potential customers do you expect to reach with your advertising? Break it down, not only by total market size, but also by segment and individual channels. There may be overlap on channels; that is normal since the same consumer uses multiple sales channels, but it should give you a clear understanding of your biggest opportunities.

- **Customers** – How many customers do you want to get? What is your total number of new customers that you expect to have? What percent do you expect to increase each month and how many return customers will you get? If your product is a 90-day supply, then expect return customers three months from initial purchase. Give a breakdown for the total number of expected customers.

- **Buying** – How often will customers purchase your product? Is it once a month, once a year, or just once, period? How much will they spend on it and what will the size of their purchase be? Could they buy multiple products at the same time? For example, when canned soup is on sale at the grocery store three for $5, I usually buy six cans of soup. That will last me two weeks before I have to go back for more. Describe how often your customers will purchase and the volume at which they do it.

What are your measureable short term and long-term objectives?

Strategy

- Describe the specific ways you'll reach your target market. What strategy will you use? Start by thinking if you'll use a mass-market approach versus a segmented approach. Mass market is where you advertise to your target market as a whole with a broad reaching advertising campaign. TV can be a mass-market approach. Segmented marketing is when you pick a specific group within your target market and advertise directly to them. A radio ad on a local sports talk show may target mostly men from 25-45 years old. Which approach will you pick?

- Profile your customer within your strategy. Describe their gender, age, income, education, lifestyle, buying patterns, attitude towards buying new products, buying ability, and even geographic region they live in. Explain how your strategy relates to these qualities.

- What are the needs of the customer? Describe what motivates the customer to go out and spend money on this product. How will your product meet these needs? How will you communicate your product's value?

- How does the customer use the product? This is the old who, what, why, when, and how question. Who is using it, why are they using it, when are they using it, what are the benefits they get from it, and how are they using it? Then describe how your product either fits or disrupts that process.

- Finally, what is the consumer's purchase process? What steps do they take in order to buy your product? Where do they start researching and get their information? How long does it take them from the time they start researching to the time they purchase? With the cans of soup, it's a few seconds versus a new house that can be several months. What goes into their decision process? Is it economic factors, trends, timing? And who makes the purchase? Is it the consumer directly, is a broker, or is it a third party? Describe the entire buying process the customer goes through and then relate it to your product. Is your product's purchase process the same, easier, or more difficult? Look for opportunities that can make the buying process easier or faster.

4. PRODUCT

Objectives

- What are my measureable short term and long-term product objectives? What is the current problem with existing products in the market? What limitations do other products have or what are they missing? Discuss what you hope to deliver that other products currently can't. How are you going to differentiate your product from others? How are you going to solve that current problem?

Strategy

- Describe current products and what they offer customers. Talk about their features, value, pricing, distribution, advertising, promotions, and things they do well. Why do customers buy them? Then discuss what value your product brings and why customers will want to buy your product. What does your product do better? How do you clearly demonstrate your product's benefits to the customer or that your product solves the problem they're facing?

- Describe the packaging you're going to design and why you picked that. Is it the same or different from competitors? What benefit does your packaging provide? How expensive is it and what message does it send the customer? Describe any details about product packaging that affects the purchase.

- Discuss your branding strategy in a short, clear, concise manner that quickly conveys your plan. Look at the ideas you came up with in chapter 6 about branding and put them in here. Talk about your logo, tagline, and message. How will your branding connect with the customer? Keep this section to about 1-2 paragraphs.

- Discuss who your competitors are and where they fit in the market. How will your product compete with them? Is it price, quality, or features? Describe the reach that your competitors have-their breadth and depth. Will you compete with them in all channels or just a few? List whom you are going up against and how you plan to compete with them.

5. PROMOTION

Objectives

- Describe your short and long-term promotion objectives. What do you want to accomplish from product promotion? Is it to increase brand awareness? This is what most startups should begin with. Is it to increase online or storefront customer traffic? Is it to improve your close rates and make your marketing more effective? Maybe it's simply to acquire new customer information through contests or surveys that you'll use later on. Your objectives can be a combination of these as well; whatever you hope to accomplish during your first year.

Strategy

- I provided a promotional tool kit below that you
  can use. This is a list of ideas to use in your
  promotion campaigns. Pick some from the list, and
  also create your own, to include in the promotional
  strategy. How are you going to reach the customer?
  This is the section to detail exactly what you're
  going to do. This will probably be the longest
  section in your marketing plan. That's fine because
  it needs to be detailed. Include a timeline for when
  you are going to use the ideas as well. Are you
  going to jump right into direct mail or wait a few
  months until you are more known? When are you
  going to use coupons? Describe the promotion
  ideas you're going to use, how you'll use them,
  when you're going to use them, and whom you're
  going to reach. Remember the S.M.A.R.T.E.R goals.
  These should be attainable and relevant. A million-
  dollar national ad campaign for your local car wash
  isn't realistic or relevant. Create a campaign that
  you can effectively do with your resources.

PROMOTION TOOL KIT			
EVERY DAY	**CAMPAIGNS**	**PUBLIC RELATION**	**COMMUNICATION**
Business cards	Email Mktg	Press release	All Social Media
Website	Content Mktg	Public	Blogs
Elevator	Contests	Events	Articles
Pitch	Advertisements	Public-	Newsletters
Brochures	Sponsorships	Speaking	Public Speaking
Surveys	Direct Mail	Public-	Webinars
	Coupons	Service	RSS Feeds
	Free Trials	Donations	Surveys
	Reward Cards		Seminars

Which One Should I Pick?

As entrepreneurs we will always struggle with finding the best return on our investment. There are so many options for advertising and promotion campaigns. Most of the times your resources will be limited and you can only pick a few. So what are the best options to choose? Email marketing? Google Adwords? Here's an example of how to measure your Return On Investment (ROI) on Promotion Campaigns.

ROI EXERCISE

PRINT ADS   ROI = $400

TOTAL ADS	# OF LEADS PER AD	10% BUY RATE	REVENUE PER SALE	TOTAL AD REVENUE	TOTAL AD COST
4	80	8	$100	$800	$400

ASSUMPTIONS:

20 leads per ad, 10% close rate, $100 avg revenue per sale, each ad costs $100

DIRECT MAIL (COLOR POST CARDS)   ROI = $1000

TOTAL PRINTED	5% EXP. REPONSE	10% BUY RATE	REVENUE PER SALE	TOTAL REVENUE	TOTAL CARD COST
5,000	250	25	$100	$2500	$1500

ASSUMPTIONS:

5% response rate, 10% close rate, $100 avg sale, $1500 costs (design, print, postage)

ONLINE PAY-PER-CLICK ADS   ROI = $0

TOTAL CLICKS	AVG COST PER CLICK	10% CLICK THRU	10% BUY RATE	TOTAL REVENUE	TOTAL COST
500	$1.00	50	5	$500	$500

ASSUMPTIONS:

$1 cost per click, 10% click thru rate, 10% close rate, $100 avg sale

Based on these examples, which promotion campaign would you choose? The direct mail has the highest ROI over the two other options. This may have been counter-intuitive to pick, because we often think of mail options as outdated. We naturally lean towards online advertising and e-commerce. Before you invest heavily in your marketing campaign, run some ROI calculations and determine which option provides the highest return. This will ensure you are getting the most out of your efforts and resources. Be sure to include these ROI models in your marketing plan to reinforce your strategy.

THERE'S MONEY IN YOUR INBOX

Expert Tip - email automation currently has the highest ROI when done correctly. Invest the time to create complete pre & post purchase email sequences, and you'll see higher conversions along with return customers.

---

6. PLACEMENT

Objectives

- What are my short and long-term objectives for placement? Is it to reach the most number of people, to reach the highest percentage of my potential customers (notice the difference), or to create partnerships with affiliates and distribution channels? What does the placement mean for your order processing? Is fulfillment longer or shorter? How will it affect my order processing accuracy and promise to customers? What image am I delivering to my customer with my placement? This relates to the example I gave of why Tiffany & Co. doesn't sell their diamonds in K-Mart. Does it affect my branding? Describe the placement of your product and why you've picked those channels.

Strategy

- Detail the sales and distribution channels you've selected. This can be Internet, retail, door-to-door, wholesalers, mail order, affiliate programs, or other channels. Discuss why you've selected these and include the expected ROI of each channel from your sales plan. Detail any affiliate programs you're using such as the type, size, cost, geographic region, and target market they reach. Discuss your distribution networks. Are they consumer direct, indirect, fulfilled by distribution centers, or based on consignment?

- Also make sure to detail your customer service plan. We haven't talked a lot about this yet, but it is key to any successful company. What policies will you have in place to take care of the customer? If there's a complaint or return, how will you handle it? Are your policies standard for the industry or something unique the customer may not be used to? Form a solid, customer-friendly plan and list it here.

7. PRICING

Objectives

- What are your short and long-term pricing goals? What pricing strategy should you use based on current market conditions and what response rate do you expect? Does your pricing strategy meet your overall financial goals? When demand or market conditions change, how flexible is your pricing model? When you adjust your pricing, how will it impact your sales and other goals?

Strategy

- Describe your price strategy in detail for each of your channels. List any discounts, free trials, subscriptions, or bundling you'll use. What are your payment terms? Do customers pay 100% upfront at the time of sale, will you have installments, or offer credit terms? If you plan on having different payment terms, break out the terms for each channel. For example, if you plan to give 60-day credit terms, what does it mean for your revenue during those 60 days? Are you able to afford overhead, costs, and expenses during that time? What happens if the buyer doesn't pay within the 60 days? Give realistic projections on how the payment terms relate to your revenue.

- Discuss how your pricing strategy can change to meet increasing or decreasing demand. When customer-buying patterns change, how will you react? Demonstrate how flexible your margins are.

8. INTEGRATED MARKETING STRATEGY

Time to get to the scary stuff. Luckily for you, I'm here to help make it simple. Create your Integrated Marketing Strategy in order to maximize your reach and sales. A good integrated plan hits customers from different angles and communicates your message in different ways. This is also referred to as <u>Omni-Channel Marketing</u>. It presents the same brand message a variety of ways, across multiple channels at once. This greatly improves brand awareness, and helps consumers become familiar with your product. As marketers, we need to provide a seamless experience to consumers, regardless of channel or device. Consumers can now interact with a company in a physical store, on an online website or mobile app, through a catalog, or through social media. They need to receive a consistent message in every channel. Using an integrated plan will help capture more customers and maximize sales.

I've created a list of marketing channels and ideas. This categorizes each action into a specific channel. It's an easy reference to see how well you are integrating your own marketing strategy. **Circle at least one item from each column**. If you make sure to implement each of the ideas, then you'll have an Integrated Marketing Plan. Simple as that!

INTEGRATED MARKETING PLAN					
ONLINE ADVERTISING	PROMOTION	TRADITIONAL ADVERTISING	PERSONAL	NETWORK	PUBLIC RELATIONS
Web Ads	Coupon	Television	Presentation	Facebook	Press
Social Ads	Rebates	Radio	Events	Twitter	Release
Banners	Free Trials	Magazines	Speaking	YouTube	Media Tour
Newsletter	Contests	Billboards	Networking	Instagram	Events
Email Mktg	Bundling	Mailers	Luncheons	Reddit	Donations
Subscription	Reward	Sponsorship	Buzz Cards	Forums	PSA
RSS Feeds	Card	Email	Thank You's	Co-ops	Press Conf.
Blogs	Discounts	Tradeshow	Door-to-door	Partnership	
				Feedback	

That's it. There's your Marketing Plan. You now have a detailed plan of attack and are ready to launch your product. Make sure you refer to this plan often and measure where you're at. It's easy to get lost in the day-to-day stress of running a company and often plans can get off track. Startups can often be confusing and you'll have an urge to change your marketing tactics often. This will keep you on track and give you a balanced strategy. I rely heavily on my marketing plan each month. Execute yours, and you'll start generating more leads and sales faster.

IT'S NOT ABOUT THE MONEY

Coca-Cola is one of the biggest and most successful companies in the world. They have also committed one of the biggest marketing mistakes - New Coke. In 1985, Coca-Cola decided to replace its established and popular Coke formula. Several blind taste tests showed consumers picked the sweeter Pepsi taste over Coke. After some product testing of their own, they decided to change their formula and launch New Coke. They did not expect the amount of backlash they received over the new product. New Coke failed to win over customers, despite a very expensive two-year marketing campaign. Coca-Cola's market research failed to show the true brand loyalty customers had for the original formula. Their product testing also failed to get useful feedback from the customer. During the testing, only a small percentage of people got to actually try the new formula and most were given a simple 'yes/no' questionnaire. In the end, Coca-Cola spent over $4 million dollars marketing New Coke with dismal results. Soon they switched back to their original Coke formula and labeled the cans Classic Coca-Cola. Sales immediately improved. New Coke was relabeled Coke II and sold in a few select markets, but was finally discontinued all together in 2002. Coke stuck with the 'Classic' label on their cans for 22 years, only removing it in 2009. This is an incredible example that shows it doesn't matter how much money you spend on a marketing campaign. The consumer ultimately decides what will sell or not. Be aware of this power in your own marketing. It took Coca-Cola 22 years to even redesign their packaging after this mistake. I encourage you to research this period in Coke's history and learn from the New Coke example.

9

YOU WILL DO EVERYTHING YOURSELF

Eight Tools You Need

As a small business owner, your business cards might as well say 'I do everything'. You'll have to get used to doing a little of everything in your company. No longer do you have accounting and HR departments. That's you now. The marketing team....you. The sales team....you. Shipping and warehouse...that's you. See where I'm going with this? There's a lot of work that goes into running a business beyond your product launch and sales. You'll spend a large portion of your time working on things other than sales or marketing. Get used to the idea that you'll spend a few all-nighters packaging a shipment or getting a promotion ready. There's no manual to tell you exactly how to handle all the intangibles, but I can give you some advice. There are a few things you should be aware of and can do now to help your-self.

Up to this point, we've discussed the more structured parts of running your business - analysis, charts, plans, and strategies. What we haven't talked about are the intangibles required for a small business. Many times you will have to be creative, self-reliant, and a jack of all trades. At some point, you will have to do everything yourself in order to meet a deadline. It requires an enormous amount of ingenuity, self-motivation, and patience.

During the startup, you'll have to rely mostly on yourself to get things done. As you progress and start to assemble a team, you'll still be required to oversee everything and fill in any gaps. It is a job that will require a lot of time and headaches. Get used to it now. Here are a few tips for things you can do to make it easier on yourself.

CONTENT MARKETING

Content marketing drives every consumer's buying experience. It is the practice of creating and sharing valuable, relevant and consistent content with your audience, and one of the most important tools you have. A solid content marketing plan should be at the core of every company. Red Bull rose to fame through content marketing. Instead of taking their enormous competitors of Coke, Pepsi, Monster and Mountain Dew head on, they developed a powerful online content strategy and overtook them all. Red Bull became a publishing company that happens to sell a beverage. They are the poster child of a brand-turned-publisher. You need to get into the same mind set. Your focus will be creating a useful content marketing strategy to connect with your customers.

Content marketing relies on giving your audience something valuable in order to build trust, brand knowledge and convert their interest into a sale. This is most often free content that you have developed, created or written. It is <u>not</u> a sales pitch for your product. Engaging content focuses on topics your customers are interested in. Perhaps your customers are into road biking. Think about all the other related topics they care about – nutrition, fitness, bike clothing and gear. That is the content you want to create; content that draws the audience into your brand. Ensure whatever you publish is relevant, interesting and adds value to your customers. Good content marketing is thought-provoking, challenges a popular belief or changes the way your customer goes about their daily life. It's visually appealing and stimulating, and creates a sense of curiosity or excitement. Publish this content in your channels consistently. You'll engage more customers and see higher conversions.

Think about some great articles or blogs that you've read recently. What made them interesting? Did they grab your attention or provide useful information? Content marketing is a powerful way to establish your brand in the market. The more consumers get use to reading or seeing your content, the more likely they are to purchase from you. Start thinking of yourself as a publisher first, that happens to sell a product.

DYNAMIC SALES

It's easy to fall back on sales channels that you're used to seeing. We're comfortable with store fronts or e-commerce websites. More established companies use those sales channels, so we tend to mimic what we see. Be bold. Look for new sales opportunities. Don't be afraid to try out new channels you're not used to, because they can lead to unexpected markets. At some point, you will feel like you're in a rut and only moving in one direction. Reaching out for new ideas can help get you out of that rut. Look for new partnerships or ways into other markets. Try to reach out from your normal sales channels and look for new ones.

Play to your strengths. As a small business, one of your advantages over larger competitors is that you are more dynamic. You can change direction and adapt faster than they can. Always make sure to stay dynamic. You want to be able to jump on a new opportunity as soon as you see it. When I played hockey growing up I had a coach tell me once that, if I could be quicker than the defender, then their size wouldn't matter. Same can be true in business. The market can move quickly. Find a way to move faster and stay ahead of it.

CUSTOMER RELATIONSHIP MANAGEMENT (CRM)

Invest in a good customer management system or CRM! You're going to put a lot of time, money, and effort into generating customers. It is imperative to have a reliable way to store, track and analyze customer information. You will use it for email campaigns, orders, customer service issues, returns, promotions, sales funnels and earning return customers. It is one of the most important tools you'll use. Spreadsheets just don't cut it anymore. Luckily for you, there are some great inexpensive software options available.

Do a simple online search for CRM software and you'll be able to compare hundreds of options. Most have very robust features like sales forecasting, email management, invoices, purchase orders, call logs, web leads, and data storage. Look for ones that include customer call back reminders, to-do-lists, and have fully automated sales sequences. Your goal is to find one that costs less than $300 per year. There are even some nice free options available. Pick one that fits your needs and business. Here are a few of the most popular ones currently.

CRM NAME	WEBSITE	COST	FEATURES
ZOHO	zoho.com	Basic – $12/mo Pro - $20/mo	Complete toolkit
ACTIVE CAMPAIGN	activecampaign.com	Basic - $9/mo Plus - $49/mo	Powerful email CRM system
SALESCLOUD	salesforce.com	Basic -$25/mo Pro - $65/mo	User friendly, Top Seller
INSIGHTLY	insightly.com	Starter – FREE Basic - $12/mo	Robust and affordable

ACCOUNTING SOFTWARE

Remember those accounting classes you zoned out on during college? Now it's time to use that information. Keeping accurate financial records is essential for forecasts and taxes. You must track sales, income, expenses, and tax deductions.

Don't risk an IRS audit. Good accounting software that's easy to use is vital to running a successful company. It's also a good idea to attend a free accounting class online or at a local community education center. At a minimum, consult with your friend who is a licensed CPA and have him give you a refresher. You'll want to have a strong understanding of business bookkeeping, because now it's up to you to keep it straight.

TITLE	FEATURES	COST
QUICKBOOKS ONLINE	Online and mobile access, sales and expense reports, complete tool kit	Simple - $10/mo Plus - $24/mo
WAVE ACCOUNTING	Cash flow, invoices, check writing, simple to use	Basic – FREE Payroll - $20/mo
ZOHO BOOKS	Connects to popular online payment gateways	Basic - $7/mo Pro - $27/mo
FRESHBOOKS	Simple and intuitive user interface, complete system	Sprout - $10/mo Popular - $30/mo

DESIGN SOFTWARE

Whether you are artistically gifted or not, you'll find yourself designing logos and images for your business. You can find freelance graphic designers on sites like Upworks.com, but a good graphic design software can save you both time and money designing images yourself, especially when you're under a time crunch to create a banner, ad or update your site. There are hundreds of design software options to choose from, both online and for your computer. Again, it may be worth taking a free graphic design course from a local community education center. Otherwise, there are lots of tutorial videos for free online. Pick a software and start practicing on it. My personal favorite is InkScape for Macs. It is a powerful and easy to use graphic design program that handles anything you need to do. I create most of my logos, design promotion images, and edit pictures on it. I'm able to create any graphic image I need. Often when an opportunity presents itself, you'll have little time to hire a professional designer. Creating your own images can mean the difference between capitalizing or missing out. Marketing will require a wide variety of images, and the more you're able to create yourself, the better.

SOFTWARE	FEATURES	PRICE
INKSCAPE	Mac-based, powerful, user friendly, uses SVG	FREE
SERIF DRAWPLUS	Simple, fast, powerful, similar to Photoshop tools	FREE
COREL PAINT SHOP	Easy to use, many editing tools	$99.99
ADOBE PHOTOSHOP & CREATIVE CLOUD	Windows based complete toolkit, sets the standard for graphic design	1 App - $20/mo All Apps – $50/mo

HOLD ON A MOMENT

Several years ago when I was starting my second company we entered the Grow America Springboard competition. They offer small business grants to startup companies. We competed against several other startups, including a friend of mine from business school. Part of the requirement was creating a 30-second video about your product and company. My friend hired a professional graphic designer to create the video for him, while I decided to take on the project myself. I put in several hours working in InkScape and iMovie and has happy with the results. My friend was not as lucky. The night before the submission deadline, his designer called to inform him he wasn't able to complete the video. He was left in a difficult position and ended up pulling an all-nighter to throw together a video. Guess who received the grant?

SHIPPING

Chances are you'll be shipping products yourself and you won't have a warehouse. Depending on the size of the product, you may even be doing the fulfillment and shipping right out of your own house. As a startup, you still want to appear as large as possible and create a professional image with the customer. Nothing says amateur more than handwritten address labels and stamps. One way to make it look like you run a large scale operation is to buy a thermal label printer and branded boxes. Thermal labels are the standard for large companies and make your shipments look professional. They are not expensive to pick up on EBay and easy to hook up to your computer. Zebra makes excellent thermal printers and I personally use their LP 2844 printer. You can currently find them online for around $100 and it adds instant credibility to your shipment.

For your packaging, buy personalized packing tape or stamps with your logo. Use this on the outside of your box. Not only does your customer know that their order has arrived, but it's free advertising to everyone that sees it in transit. Have you ever ordered from Nuts.com? If not, then do a quick online image search of their packaging. Their boxes are an extension of their branding and a form of marketing. Make sure your packaging reflects your branding as well.

COMPANY	PRODUCT	DETAILS
ZEBRA	Thermal label printers	2844 or other models online
U-LINE	Shipping supplies	Boxes, bubble wrap, tape
USPS, FEDEX, UPS	Shipping services	Price shop based on shipping location, weight, and size
VISTAPRINT	Branding supplies	Business cards, flyers, inserts

EMAILS AND SURVEYS

What better way to stay in touch with your customers than sending special offers, promotions, thank you notes, and surveys. Thankfully, there are several great free services you can use to do this. If the CRM you purchased does not include customer contact features, check out these sites. Post purchase communication is a vital part of customer retention and these services make it easy. Make sure to utilize these as part of your marketing plan.

COMPANY	SITE	SERVICE
SURVEY MONKEY	www.surveymonkey.com	Free online customer surveys
MAIL CHIMP	www.mailchimp.com	Free email marketing
SURVEY GIZMO	www.surveygizmo.com	Free surveys

PATIENCE

I can't tell you where to find this one, but you're going to need a lot of it. I've literally spent an entire day trying to get a simple 9-digit routing number from my merchant service provider. Eight hours spent just on that. Running a business is complicated. You are going face a variety of challenges thrown at you every day. Simple things always seem to take longer than you expect and complicated things never get done fast enough. You are going to need a lot of patience to get through this. Remind yourself why you started your own business and the goals you want to accomplish. As I mentioned in the beginning, starting a business will put a strain on the relationships you have. Startup businesses are stressful and require a lot of work. Every entrepreneur goes through ups and downs. The more patience you have will make this adventure easier on you.

10

THE $100 PROFESSIONAL WEBSITE

Build An Online Presence Like A Pro

Websites are a must for businesses, even if you have a physical storefront. A website can be the most common connection with customers you'll have. The Internet is easily accessible, inexpensive, has a broad reach, and often is the first place customers turn to for information. Yet many companies do not spend the little effort required to have a professional-looking website. How many times have you visited a site that is cluttered, uninformative, or difficult to navigate? And how long do you stay on that site? Customer's attention spans' are short when browsing the Internet, so you've got to grab their attention as soon as they hit your site. Call this the 10 Second Rule. You have 10 seconds to capture their attention and tell them what you do. If you can't do that, they're gone. A poorly designed website can drive away customers, just as a well-built site can attract them. It's so important to have an effective website. Luckily, it's not hard to do.

Websites give you an online identity. They reflect your branding and message. Think of your website as a full time sales agent talking to a customer. What would you want that sales agent to say? Your website should be clear, be easy to navigate/understand, present the key information, create confidence with the customer, have a call-to-action, and direct the customer to buy. Even if you are only planning on running a storefront operation, an effective website will help drive traffic to you. Consumers do the majority of their research online and decide what to buy before they even leave the house. The days of window-shopping are over. You need to have a presence online. Thankfully, there are simple programs and easy-to-use resources available to create your entire online site. There's no excuse for having a bad website.

You can easily spend thousands of dollars on building a website. Most professionally built sites cost upwards of $15,000. I'll show you the way to do it for under $100. The main purpose of your website is to convert hard earned consumer traffic into actual sales. Let's go through a few of these simple steps to building an effective website.

1. **BUY A DOMAIN NAME** – If you haven't already, you need to pick a domain name. For you newbies, that's the www.mycompany.com part. You'll want to choose some

options that represent your company, service, or product to the consumer and are easy to remember. Short one or two word names are the best. They can be your company name, a catchy phrase, or anything that grabs the customer's attention. Then you need to research if it's available for purchase. Sites, like Go Daddy, Name Cheap or Network Solutions, allow you to search domain names and tell you if they're available or not. Dot coms and dot nets are the most commonly used, however consumers are also becoming accustomed to dot co and dot org. I would stick to finding a dot-com name, unless you have specific strategy for another domain ending. Domains cost you about $13 per year to purchase, although, with various promotions can be found for as little as $1 per year.

2. **FIND A HOSTING COMPANY** – Once you have your domain name, you need to find a site that will host your website. Think of this like parking garage. They store your website and keep it safe. Again, there are hundreds of hosting companies fighting for your business. Go Daddy is one of the largest ones and whom I personally use. They offer a variety of services at low prices and have a high dependability rate. Hosting your site will cost about $5-$10 per month. At the time of printing this book Go Daddy was offering a promotion for a free domain name, basic website with five pages, one email address, and hosting for

$1/month! You can create a professional-looking website from their templates and have it online for only $12 per year. Go Daddy's premium package that includes an SSL certificate to protect consumer credit card information during transactions is only $8/mo. Hosting companies make it incredibly easy to get a professional-looking website quickly. Bluehost is also a trusted favorite my company's site is hosted with.

3. **DESIGN YOUR SITE** – I just mentioned Go Daddy templates for creating your site, but there are plenty of other great options. WordPress is a standard website platform used, and one I'd recommend. They are the best at content publishing, and offer free themes and templates you can use (http://wordpress.org/extend/themes). Simply plug in your content and pictures into the template, and you are done. Best of all, many are preconfigured mobile responsive which is critical for SEO results.

If you're looking for a template with more features or e-commerce specific, simply search website templates online or check out Site Builder (www.sitebuilder.com). Their templates are designed for hundreds of different categories to give you a specific look and feel. You can also choose from E-commerce, Magneto, Shopify, WooCommerce, Presta Shop, Big Commerce, Zen Cart, and

OpenCart themes for online shopping carts. These have the shopping cart, checkout, and SEO plug-ins built right into them. Site Builder gives you a free domain, free template and free builder tools. Pro hosting plans start at $10/mo. This is well worth the investment for a professional-looking site.

4. **WRITING CONTENT** – This may sound like the most difficult part, but with a little guidance you can write great content for your site. You don't need to be a professional writer. Effective websites follow similar patterns and writing styles, because that is what converts. Start by looking at several sites you like. Get a feel for their layout. What information do they present, in what order and what are their calls-to-action? See the style?

The secret to writing great content for your website is to keep it clear, concise, personal and highlight your value. A simple format is to call attention to a problem your consumer faces. Then present how your product solves that problem. Search for the true value you offer consumers. What truly motivates a person to buy your product? Make sure to describe that in your content.

K.I.S.S. – Keep It Simple Stupid

A common mistake I often see, is companies get too technical. Consumers do not care about the deeply technical aspects of your product. They want to know what it can do for them. Focus on the benefits more than the features. When describing features, keep it simple and geared for your mainstream audience.

Finally, don't forget your call to action. What action do you want your customers to do after reading your site? Purchase online, contact you or go to your store? Ensure your call to action is clear, easy to follow and located on multiple pages of your site.

If you're still not sure about writing content, simply Google 'sales copy writing'. A list of how-to articles is available on tips to creating compelling content that converts. After all, that is the purpose of your site.

Once you've designed your site test it out to make certain you capture the customer's attention. Show it to several friends and let them look at it for 10 seconds. Then ask them what your product, branding, message, and value are. If they can't tell you what it is you do, then your content isn't effective. Make sure to highlight your value right away on the site. Pick content that resonates with the customer, but make sure to keep the content relevant and on message. Again, just because it resonates well with you doesn't mean it attracts the customer. Go through these tests until you're satisfied with the results. A good landing page will engage your customer and explain what your product does in a glance.

5. **MERCHANT SERVICES** – This use to be a very complicated area of business selecting the right merchant service provider. A merchant service is the company that processes the payment. They securely collect the customer credit card information and charge them for the product. When I published the first edition of this book, there were few options to choose from. They were expensive and frustrating to deal with. Thankfully, since then the merchant service industry has completely changed and there are many more business-friendly options to choose from.

   • Stick to a single merchant service that does everything for you and only takes a percentage of the sale. Companies, like PayPal and Square, make it easy to sign up for, provide great customer service, and collect a percent of the purchase price. You only get charged when you sell something and they take it out of the revenue. This makes it simple and helps you avoid unnecessary monthly costs.

- Go mobile! Even if you are running retail locations and need a credit card processing machine, look into a mobile credit card processing solutions. Companies, like Square Up, PayPal, and Intuit offer mobile devices that plug into smart phones and tablets. They are simple to use, small, portable, inexpensive, and a great business tool. Plus, they automatically link to most accounting software! They typically have the lowest processing fees, plus you can get the card reader and app for free. There are even tablet stands and money drawers that sync with your tablet and operate exactly as a register would.

- Avoid costly and confusing merchant services that charge you monthly or have gateway fees. There are better solutions available. Break out of the mindset that you need a traditional cash register and credit card machine. Take a moment to research solutions that would work for your business. You'll end up saving yourself a lot of money and headaches.

6. **PROMOTE YOUR SITE** – Now that you have your website up, it's time to get your site noticed. First, register your site with a number of free search engine registrations and online directories. Search engines, like Google, Yahoo, Bing, Alexa, Entireweb.com, About.com, Ask.com, and AOL, have free registrations. They want to know who you are and the registration process is easy. This will ensure your website is listed in search results. To get towards the top of those search results is a much more complex challenge that we'll talk about next. For now, you are on your way and customers can find you.

For as little as $96, you just created a professional-looking website with a shopping cart and secure checkout that will get noticed. Congratulations! Don't forget to customize your confirmation and thank you emails that customers receive after the purchase. As we'll discuss its important to build your post purchase email funnels. It is often a missed opportunity to build your brand community and create lifelong customers. You are now ready to launch your website!

As you grow, you may decide to hire a web designer. A good web designer can definitely add customized features and style to your site. However, they come at a high cost. Good web designers can charge anywhere from $50-$200 per hour and a project can easily run several thousand dollars. Plus, skilled web designers are in high demand and likely to have bigger clients than you. They are a business too, so it's not uncommon to have your project put on hold while they finish the more lucrative project. This lost time can be costly and frustrating. I've done my share of waiting for web projects to be finished and can tell you that it is extremely aggravating.

There are also resources available, like **Freelancer.com** and **Upwork.com**, offering a wide variety of services from freelance professionals all over the world. You post your project and freelancers bid on the job. Then you award the job to the best bid, ensuring you get the price you are looking for. I've used Upwork.com to complete a few projects above my expertise. It can be a great way to get a project done cheaply, but be aware of a few risks. These developers are also running multiple projects at the same time. Attention to detail can sometimes be an issue or they miss deadlines. I've had multiple developers 'go dark' after starting a project and disappear. Since they often are in other countries, you can't swing by their office. Nothing is more frustrating than waiting several weeks, only to restart the project and search process. Also, the lowest bids often come from overseas developers in Indonesia, India, or Vietnam. Language and cultural barriers may become a challenge. Their grammar and code writing may be very different from ours in the United States creating errors. If you decide to hire a freelancer to help, make certain you are communicating clearly and regularly throughout the project to ensure it gets done. On a limited budget, these services can really help you out.

Our next step is to drive traffic and customers to your site. This is when you start monitoring analytics and measuring results. Your goal is to maximize your conversion rates and generate sales. Time to start making money.

LEAVE IT ALONE

As business owners, it is easy to obsess about every little detail. Nothing will ever be exactly right. One of the worst mistakes you can make is attempting to change your website before a big marketing event. My lesson-learned-moment came the night before my company was going to be featured on a morning TV show. The show's main viewership was our target market, so we expected a spike in website traffic. My team had discussed a shopping cart change of offering customers a subscription option. Instead of full payment, they could spread the purchase price out over three payments. The e-commerce plugin looked simple to install and we thought it would be a great idea to have the option ready for the TV show. You can probably guess what happened next. Not only was the plugin not easy to install, but it crashed our entire shopping cart. Code from another plugin mixed with this plugin and the results were catastrophic. We pulled an all-nighter trying to fix the issue without any success. We even hired a developer overseas - 2 AM in the United States was 11 AM there - who collected a nice rush delivery fee, but wasn't able to get it fixed in time either. The TV show did provide a nice spike in our web traffic. We saw about 2,000 visitors that morning and we made zero sales. Our effort to make last minute improvements wasted a wonderful marketing opportunity. The lesson is to leave your website alone before a big event. The risks are greater than the rewards.

11

BUILD YOUR OWN SEO CAMPAIGN

The World Of Search Engines Made Simple

SEO stands for Search Engine Optimization and is a process to maximize your visibility online. It is the roadway that directs customers to your site and, when done correctly, will have a major impact on your revenue. You will hear a lot of opinions about the best SEO methods, but the truth is nobody, except the search engines themselves, know the exact formula for maximizing your SEO results. Search engines have hundreds of ranking factors and will continually change their formulas, altering the best methods. SEO is not overly difficult, but it is an evolving process that takes time and dedication. Professional firms charge a lot of money to run your SEO campaigns, so I'll show you how to build a successful SEO strategy yourself. I'll also give you the latest tips from SEO professionals and the two most important factors for a winning SEO strategy. Finally, we'll discuss how to stay current with the best SEO methods in order to keep those rankings you worked hard for.

You've done the difficult part in your Marketing Plan on where to find your customers online. Now it's time to attract their attention and drive traffic to your product. Welcome to the world of SEO.

Search engines currently rely heavily on finding unique, quality and relevant content to rank your website in a list of search results. Successful SEO campaigns are built around well written and engaging content for their audience. Your goal should be getting ranked on the first page of search results, because honestly how often do you search beyond the first two or three pages? Companies try a wide variety of tactics to achieve this, however most SEO campaigns fail, because the company lacks knowledge and discipline to see their plan through. The strategy I'm about to lay out for you focuses on creating high quality content to drive your SEO results. Once you start, trust in the process and be consistent. In a competitive market, it takes great content and patience to climb into the top results.

PLATFORMS & PLUGINS

Earlier, I recommended using WordPress for your website platform and here's why. WordPress was originally designed as a blog post software, and is currently the best website platform for publishing content. Now you may be asking, "why do I want to spend time publishing content when my goal is to sell product?". In order to run a successful SEO campaign, you need to start thinking of yourself as a content publisher first. We will discuss this strategy in much greater detail later in this chapter and also future chapters. Consumers are searching for products and information related to their specific needs. Search engines understand this and factor in the quality, originality and relevance of content for overall ranking results. The better the content, the higher your search results are going to be. WordPress platforms make it very simple to publish new material, manage your content and receive user-generated content.

WordPress themes have many SEO features built right in, including many that are mobile friendly plus have a wide variety of plug-in options available. Plugins are additional tools that integrate into your website for added features or function. These premade plugins come in very handy and make your life simpler. They are simple to integrate and dramatically improve your site. One plugin I'd recommend using, if you're on WordPress, is Yost. Yost is a valuable SEO plugin tool that automatically adds searchable content, based on keywords you list. It's a very simple tool to use and writes all the code for you. Download the plugin and start entering your keywords to make your site more visible.

WordPress platforms are also extremely simple and intuitive to use. They do not require custom coding or programming knowledge to create new pages, edit your site or update content. With a little knowledge, this will save you a lot of time and money while working on your site. Choosing a premade WordPress template makes a lot of sense during startup. They are cost effective, the code is well designed, they are tested, content is simple to publish and they are search engine friendly. Custom building a website will be costlier, take longer, and may not deliver any better search results. Don't spend your money on this yet. Keep it simple and start with the right platform.

KEYWORDS & TITLE TAGS

Keyword based SEO strategies are outdated and dying quickly. Even just a few years ago, keywords meant everything to SEO and listing thousands of keywords was the common practice for high rankings. Search engines would collect data about a site solely based on those keywords. That's no longer the truth. Now, search engines search for relevance and meaning in your titles, content and website itself. Google, for example, scans your site for information, then interprets that data to form its own conclusions if your site is relevant to the search. It focuses more on the meaning of words, rather than the words themselves. Google also analyzes possible synonyms for searches and lists any content it believes could be related to the search. That means any search remotely related to your product could list you in the search results, with the right content on your site. Search engines are becoming incredibly sophisticated in order to deliver more relevant and interesting content to the customer. Therefore, it is far more important to create quality content on your website with a specific meaning rather than a list of phrases or keywords. Simply listing keywords is almost obsolete and a waste of time.

CONTENT MARKETING

As I discussed earlier, Content Marketing is the largest single driver in marketing today. I cannot understate the importance of creating a solid content marketing strategy, and committing yourself to it. Content marketing focuses on creating and publishing valuable, relevant and brand consistent content in order to create a relationship with your audience. It is the art of communicating with your customers without selling. Good content marketing will go beyond simply grab people's attention, and consistently engage them with your brand. Quality content marketing is at the core of every SEO strategy.

A successful SEO campaign relies on strong content marketing. Search engines are constantly scouring the internet analyzing content. Establish a content strategy around your products and top subject material. Publish blogs, articles, whitepapers, reports and even webinars in your content channels. Your content channels will include social media, YouTube, website, email campaigns and affiliate or 3rd party sites. Create strong titles and content that is relevant to your product, but also interesting to your audience. As consumers, we have many interests and influences that go into every decision we make. Knowing who your customer is, think of other interests they have beyond your product. If you manufacture sleeping bags, what other topics are your customers interested in? The environment,

National Parks, recreation, eating healthy, camping gear....the list of relevant topics can go on.

Remember, content marketing is not about selling but creating engaging content consumers are searching for. Search engines determine how relevant your content is to the search criteria. The more your post is read or shared, the higher relevancy or interest it has with readers and therefore will be ranked higher. New and regular content creation shows search engines that your site is alive and active. Search engines recognize fresh content on a continual basis and will result in better website rankings. Especially if that content is shared by others, thus creating powerful links search engines value. This leads us into our next topic.

LINK BUILDING

Several years ago, search engines looked at the number of links your site had to and from other webpages. They considered this number to be a reflection of how relevant or popular your content was. Sadly, people took advantage of this and built thousands of low quality links from their site. You could pay a freelancer $20 to build thousands of links to your site, using software. Search engines quickly adapted to this and changed their algorithms. Building high-quality links to and from other quality sites is still vital, but now they must be built organically.

Some of the best ways to do this are guest write articles or blogs for large publications, provide industry related interviews and partner with large influencers to build backlinks to your site. These links help search engines determine the overall relevance of your page, and where you should land in their rankings. They look at the number of links pointing to your page from reputable external websites in order to determine the quality of your site. If you socialize with a group of celebrities, the more likely others will believe that you are also a celebrity. The same principle is true for links. This method can also result in referral traffic to your site, from customers who trust the other site. Good link building will result in higher SEO rankings and can help establish your brand as an authority in your industry.

HUMAN INFLUENCE

There are people behind those online searches. Search engines recognize keywords, phrases and even synonyms to return a relevant match. They monitor social media, blogs, articles, websites and forums for content. In order to be recognized in searches, you have to know what your customers are looking for and talking about. First, make a list of keywords to focus on with your content. Enter potential topics into Google's Keyword Planner tool. That will give you a free list of how many times that term was searched. Select the best-related keywords to use as headlines, titles, social posts, meta-descriptions and content. Keyword sites, such as SEMRush, will even tell you if they predict a keyword to grow in popularity.

Next, make sure your content is easily sharable. Google has stated they consider content sharing as a validation of quality. They reveal very little about their actual search algorithms, so this is important to take note of. The more your content is shared, the larger impact on your SEO it will have. Utilize social sharing buttons or plug-ins on all of your content, so readers can quickly share it with others. Build internal links from posts to key pages on your site. This can quickly increase your website traffic. The more you appeal to the people searching, the better SEO results you'll have.

MOBILE INPUT

Every year we spend more and more time glued to our smart phones. We use mobile devices for everything from shopping, research, directions and online browsing. As a direct result, search engines place more relevance on mobile optimized websites and search results. In January 2016, Google made mobile optimization part of their guidelines, and uses that as a significant ranking factor. It is critical to ensure your site is mobile friendly.   A website is considered mobile friendly when content is presented well the device, does not need additional pinching or zooming to read, is easy to navigate with one finger and is properly understood by Google.

If you chose a WordPress template that is mobile friendly, then most of this is already optimized for you including the responsive design. However, there are several elements you need to avoid adding on your site. Stay away from Adobe Flash Player, as many mobile devices cannot play it. Also, stay away from using external plug-ins such as Silverlight, Java, QuickTime or Skype Click to Call as they also cause problems. Search engines recognize this and will ultimately hurt your rankings.

The subject of mobile optimization for SEO results can become a complex subject. These are the fundamentals you need to practice. As your company grows, it would be wise to consult a professional web designer to ensure your site is meeting all the mobile requirements.

VIDEO CONTENT

YouTube is the second largest search engine behind Google, yet most business owners don't think of creating video content in order to get SEO results. The truth is, people are consuming video more than ever and producing quality videos should be part of your SEO strategy. You don't need to be Steven Spielberg though to make a great video. A quick informational or how-to guide is an excellent way to introduce customers to your product, show your product in action or give answer frequently asked questions. You can even provide free information on topics related to your product or industry. Here are best practices for creating a professional looking video.

First, make sure your video is on topic, relevant, and interesting for the audience. Discuss new information, solve a common problem customers ask or just create something engaging. Remember to have your product, company, contact information or call to action clearly displayed on the video. Let people know the next step they need to take, how to reach you or how to purchase. Keep your video short, or under 5 minutes long as a best practice. I prefer keeping clips to 90 seconds as our consumer attention span shrinks.

Once it's finished, test the video out on a few friends for feedback. Does it deliver the message you intended? Was it clear, engaging and entice them to click your call-to-action? If so, then it's ready to post.

If you haven't created a YouTube or Vimeo account, it's easy to do so. YouTube simply uses your Gmail account to login. Next, build your profile and upload the video.   Use titles and sub-titles that are clear, easy to understand what the video is about, and contains relevant keywords. Make the titles descriptive, and avoid misleading titles that trick the audience into clicking your video. That will lead to negative rankings. Keep your titles short to 70 characters or less, in order for Google to display them correctly.

Finally, create interesting two sentence descriptions about your video. Give an accurate summary of what your video presents or solves for the audience. Include more relevant keywords in the description, along with links to your website and other social media pages. Remember to include a clear call-to-action in your video and description. Fill out the keywords field with your most important keywords, and select an interesting thumbnail for your video clip. That's it. You are ready to post and start building your SEO rankings with video content.

PLAY THE GAME

Like it or not, Google is currently the king of online search engines. Their policies, formulas, and search results drive what we do as companies. In order to get the best results from your strategy, you must also play the game. Thankfully, Google makes it very easy to integrate your strategy into their universe. They have complete tutorials on using their tools, plus you can usually integrate everything you need using one account. Think of this as accessorizing your company with Google products. Sign up for a Google+ account to create a business page. Build your network from friends, co-workers, and other companies in the industry. Really branch out with your network and try to reach as many people as you can.

If you have a physical storefront or business location, register with Google Places for Business and Google+ Local. This gets your business included on Google Maps and in local search results. This is key for a potential customer driving around and searching on their mobile device. Now you'll be listed in their results.

Next, create a Google AdWords account. This is your online advertising center to run ad campaigns, monitor results, and track analytics. If you are interested in publishing a blog, then link it to a Google Authorship account. Blogs can be a great way to reach your target audience with a non-sales approach. Google Authorship links your Google+ account to your blog that is also linked to your e-commerce site. See how this web is weaved together? One of Google's goals (say that five times fast!) is to rank relevant information from real people and sources. In order to verify real sources, they look for personal accounts and other user generated content. If you have your personal accounts and blogs linked to your website, it reflects well. Google is more likely to consider your e-commerce site valid and trustworthy.

Utilize Google's Keyword Planner, Trends, Alerts and Consumer Survey Tools. These are free resources they provide to lure you into their world, and help make optimizing your site incredibly easy. These tools will provide insight into your market and help keep in touch with consumer behavior.

Finally, you can create a page in Google's shopping engine. This is a page where you can list each of your products for sale. While this site itself may not generate sales directly, your Google shopping engine page adds more information to online search results. Instead of just having a website link in the search results, now your individual products, prices, and descriptions can be displayed. Play the game and utilize all of Google's tools. They certainly help add visibility to your site.

PAY PER CLICK (PPC)

PPC ads are one of the quickest ways to get your name on top search result pages. They are also one of the most difficult to get positive returns from without being experienced with paid ads. PPC is essentially a pay-for-popularity program. You pay for your higher rankings. It is important to note this is not the same as organic rankings and SEO practices we've been discussing. Your ranking will drop just as quickly when you turn off the spend. My advice is to start with a small budget of $500 or less for you to run paid ads each month. Hire a professional firm when you're ready to move above that amount. Here are the essential steps in creating a successful PPC campaign.

With any PPC ads, you assign prices to each keyword and an overall spending cap. Google ranks your price and budget against what others are willing to pay for the same space. Your ad is then placed accordingly for where your price lands you. The more you are willing to pay-per-ad click, the higher you're ranked. Choosing the right keywords and description is the key to a successful PPC campaign. The challenge is finding the highest return for your budget. If you are in a competitive market, then you're small PPC budget is going up against much larger budgets. Big companies have the ability to spend more just to be in a top position. You do not have that luxury. Here are some key points in running a successful PPC campaign:

- As we've been talking about for several chapters now, content is king. Write ad content that is engaging. Grab people's attention right from the start with a good title. Make the title and description accurate, interesting and simple. Get people curious about your ad or product, so they want to click on your link to see more. Do a quick search for the best ways to write titles for examples of current methods that are seeing results.

- Use Google Keywords tool to search relevant keywords, how many searches those words have, and a current price for the top spot. This is where you need to be creative. Look for keywords that reach your target market, but may not be the highest price ones. Select keywords that give you more exposure for a lower price. Instead of just paying for the most popular keyword, create a more effective campaign. Target words and phrases that most accurately describe your product. Your goal is to maximize your budget. Use these keywords in your titles and ads. Your titles should clearly communicate your message in a few words. A successful PPC campaign is much more than just picking popular keywords; it's about picking the *right* keywords. Here's a pop quiz for you:

You just opened a small medical clinic specializing in knee surgeries. You do a keyword search for 7 words you like and here are the results:

KEYWORDS	MONTHLY SEARCHES	PRICE PER CLICK
DOCTOR	3,500,000	$5.25
SURGEON	3,100,000	$4.80
SURGERY	2,500,000	$3.10
KNEE SURGERY	1,900,000	$2.60
ACL	1,700,000	$2.50
KNEE REPLACEMENT	1,100,000	$1.90
MEDICAL CLINIC	300,000	$0.50

Which keyword should you choose? Do you automatically go with the highest number of searches? Look for what gives you the best results at the lowest price. The keyword 'doctor' reaches 3.5 million people overall for $5.25 per click. However, are all those people looking for a knee surgeon? Probably not. The keywords 'knee surgery' and 'ACL' reach 3.6 million people for $5.10 per click combined. Plus, these are much more specific to your practice and you are reaching people that are actually looking for a knee surgeon. Don't automatically discount keywords further down the list. They may provide better results and reach more customers for a lower price.

- Before you spend any money, it's important to select a goal for your PPC campaign. What do you want to accomplish? Create a solid plan to achieve that. The most common goal of a PPC campaign is sales and conversion. It's important to decide what web page your ad is directing customers to. Sending customers directly to a product page on your website typically has the highest conversion, or chance of making a sale. Simply sending them to your home page may be too passive, and that customer will bounce. If your product is more complex or technical, then consider sending any clicks to simply informational page with a purchase or CTA (Call-To-Action) button on it. Clearly define your goals and road map first.

- Next, define a budget for your PPC campaign. How much can you afford to spend on advertising? Remember, these ads do not directly relate to sales. Do not assume you're going to get a sale for every click or for every 100 clicks. PPC campaigns are a method to direct traffic to your site. Those clicks could come from competitors wishing to run up your expenses. Set a budget that you can afford. Start out small and monitor it each day. Measure your actual conversion rates for number of sales per hundred clicks. Then adjust your budget properly. Google tends to also rank higher budgets higher. Instead of starting at $5, set your budget at $100 and see what results you get from that. I personally found that PPC budgets go much quicker than expected and offered one of my lowest ROI's.

- Test, test and retest. It's critical to monitor and analyze your ad performance daily. Perform A/B testing with different ads and audiences to see which ads are performing the best. Often simple rewording can have drastic results. A typical A/B test size will be 500-1000 impressions in order to make an educated decision. In addition, make certain you have correct spelling. You do not want any typos or embarrassing mistakes on paid advertisements. A misspelled word can negatively impact your campaign. Once you have your ad written, it is time to pick out prices and keywords.

- While Google PPC ads are currently the most popular, don't forget about other search engine PPC services. Search engines, like Bing or Yahoo, offer some excellent SEO services that can reach your customers and often at a lower price. Explore other PPC options and you may find those same keywords are cheaper. Even though Google is the 800-pound gorilla in the room, don't forget about the other 500-pound gorillas. These services can offer advantages that Google can't. Bing, for example, is fully integrated with Facebook. If your target market uses

Facebook often, then Bing may be a better PPC option to reach your customers.

- Finally, monitor your PPC campaigns constantly and make regular adjustments. Look for which ads are giving you the highest conversion rate instead of the higher click-through-rate. The higher conversion rate indicates you are reaching customers willing to buy. Take a look at your analytics daily and optimize your ads on a regular basis to achieve the best results.   You are after the highest ROI and only with consistent attention will you achieve that. Be smart with your PPC campaign and you'll see good results.

WEBMASTER TOOLS

My final SEO tip is to get a Webmaster Toolkit. These are easy and free from the major search engines. Google, Bing, and even WordPress have one you can use. Webmaster Toolkits help provide detailed reports about site traffic, ways to improve your site and ads, plus other useful information about consumer traffic patterns. Using a Webmaster Toolkit lets you quickly see ways to improve your PPC campaign and website. They are very useful tools that help to make your job easier. With a little effort and consistent monitoring, you can run a successful SEO campaign. There are lots of free plugins, tools, and information available that make it easy for you. Use them regularly and watch your search engine results climb higher and higher each month.

12

SOCIAL MEDIA

Why It Won't Work

Social media is currently one of the fastest growing marketing tools in the world. Why? The human desire to share everything with everyone. Social media offers a way to connect with millions of potential customers. Social media is dynamic, engaging, user generated, and real time. Messages and content can be spread within nano-seconds. Best of all, it's free! Yet most businesses see little to no success with social media. The reason is because people want to believe that social media is a sales tool. It's not. Facebook may have one billion users, but 999.9 million of those don't care about you. If you treat social media as a sales channel and expect to see sales increase as a result, I have a news flash - it won't work for you. So just get that out your head right now. Social media is content-driven connection with your customers. It's a way to share information, create new content, and receive feedback. Social media influences the way people think, shop, and make decisions. Your goal is to find the 1% of people on social media that do care about you. If you use social media the right way, you'll see enormous payoffs. So what is the right way? Let's discuss social media.

Customers today want to get to know your company before they purchase from you. They want to know who you are, what you're about, your company story and what motivates you. Think of this like dating. Before getting married you must get to know each other. Social media allows customers to engage with a company on a personal level. Social media lets you talk to your audience on a regular basis without the pressure of a sales pitch. It's about having a conversation and attracting consumers to your brand; drawing them in to your community and building trust. Social media campaigns also let you introduce new topics and valuable content on a regular basis, that may otherwise clutter up your website. A well run social media campaign generates clicks or traffic, and directs it back to your website and product pages. This is the top of your sales funnel.

First, you need to create a social media strategy. Every business will have a different strategy and goals. There are three main strategy categories that you first need to pick from. Is your goal to create **Brand Awareness**, improve **Sales Conversion**, or increase **Customer Loyalty**? Start with a clear direction in mind and build your strategy around that. It's important to know what you want your social media to accomplish. Picking the right goal will determine how you'll engage your customer and the type of content you post. With each of these, relevant and interesting content is important. You never want to overload people with posts or dull information. That will end your social media campaign before it starts. Studies show posting 3 times per week converts better for new brands better than every day. Ok, so you've got your goal picked out. Now to start building your campaign.

There are lots of different social media channels. Facebook, Twitter, Instagram, Flickr, YouTube, Reddit, LinkedIn, Pinterest, and Google+ are some of the more popular channels. If you are not familiar with what these are then do a little research first to understand the differences. A successful social media campaign needs to be targeted by selecting the right channel. A shotgun approach of just firing out posts and ads won't work. You need a specific target to aim for. Look back at your consumer profile and analysis from chapter 1. Who are your customers and what are their needs? How old are they, where is their location, what are their economic forces? This will determine which channel you use. Outline your customers' needs along with where they spend their time online. Pick 2-3 social media outlets that most interest your target market. Don't choose all the channels, because then you risk diluting your message and impact. Pick the most relevant ones.

It's important to note there are two types of social media posts. Free posts and paid ads. We'll discuss both types in this chapter. Both are similar with your strategy and approach. Often you'll use the same content or subject for both. Free posts typically receive "likes" or are shared with others. They are great for building an audience profile, starting conversations and spreading your brand image. Paid ads are intended to generate clicks that direct the audience to a sales or product page on your website. Anyone who clicks that ad is expressing interest in that subject and taken to a special offer. The goal of paid ads is conversion. The goal of free posts is brand awareness, engagement and audience building. The strategy outlined here applies to both, but I'll make reference to both types.

Make your content relevant and engaging. The power of social media is connecting with customers in real time. You need to be current with the content you are posting. Be agile and dynamic when creating your content. Take advantage of trends and popular issues. Consumers are more likely to pay attention to those posts. Be careful not to go overboard though. Here are three rules to follow when creating social media content:

1. Make your content unique. Don't rehash what everyone else is saying. Write about what interests you. This is an opportunity to share your value and what differentiates you.

2. Be consistent - both with your message and your postings. Your message should always revolve around your value proposition. Even in discussions people should understand your stance and get a sense of your

values. Also, be consistent with your postings. Post on a regular schedule designed to keep fresh information in front of them without overloading them. Create a post schedule with topics to outline the flow and timing.

3. Write something worthwhile. As social media becomes overloaded with information, the importance of quality content is rising. Make sure your content is interesting and of good quality. Anything less and consumers will move on to the next post.

4. Create clear action. Your posts should accomplish a specific action. Building brand awareness, generating new likes, creating conversations or driving traffic back to your website. Successful social marketing campaigns have very clear call-to-action strategies.

Don't forget to create video content as well. Video content is more popular than ever, and sites like YouTube and Vimeo are exploding. YouTube is the 2nd largest search engine, and even making changes to become more of social networking site. Videos are naturally engaging with the consumer. Ask yourself a question. Do static word posts go viral or do videos go viral? People love video content and the more you have will give you a greater opportunity to reach a broader audience. Remember, content rules. Make it unique and reflect your value proposition. Finally, remember to include your name or way for customers to find you. After all, the purpose of social media is to connect your branding with consumers. Make sure they know who you are.

Now get it out there. Share what you have to say. Direct people back to a specific product opt-in page for higher conversions, rather than your website home page. Start to develop relationships with consumers. Boost posts that generating positive responses with a few dollars. A great way to build your following and brand awareness quickly is with giveaways. Everyone loves something for free, so in order to draw attention to yourself, create small giveaways periodically. Create incentives for your viewers. People will respond to it and you'll watch the number of likes go up.

Finally, monitor your social media pages. In addition to Google Analytics, which you should be using everyday by now, I've listed several social media monitoring tools below to make this job easier. Watch the numbers and trends throughout the day to see how well your campaign is doing. Record the results, so you can track them. Be patient with your social media campaign. Remember, it's a focused effort that needs to be consistent. After a couple months, you can start tweaking your strategy, introducing new ideas, and fine-tune the campaign. At first, it may seem like a daunting task to monitor all your social media channels. User interaction is constantly changing.

However, here are several easy tools to help monitor your success. These will make your life so much easier, so get accustomed to using social media marketing tools.

20 TOP SOCIAL MEDIA SITES DESCRIPTION OR TAGLINE	
FACEBOOK	Facebook helps you connect and share with the people in your life.
BLOGGER	Blogger to give you an easy way to share your thoughts
TWITTER	Find out what's happening, right now, with the people and organizations you care about.
WORDPRESS	WordPress is web software you can use to create a beautiful website or blog.
LINKEDIN	Be great at what you do.
PINTEREST	Organize and share things you love.
GOOGLE+	With Google+, you can share the right things with the right people.
FLIKR	The home for all your photos.
YOUTUBE	Broadcast Yourself
TUMBLR	Tumblr lets you effortlessly share anything.
WIKIA	Create. Collaborate. Be Original.
REDDIT	Reddit is a website about everything
INSTAGRAM	Fast beautiful photo sharing

BEBO	It is your life online -- a social experience that helps you discover what's going on with your world.
XING	Success is best when shared with others.
TAGGED	The social network for meeting new people.
MEETUP	Neighbors getting together to learn something, do something, share something...
ORKUT	Get the conversation started.
RENREN	Chat with fun new people, share photos and interests, even date!
FOURSQUARE	Foursquare helps you and your friends make the most of where you are.

SOCIAL MEDIA MARKETING TOOLS

While social media can help increase traffic to your website, very few businesses actually use it successfully and increase sales. Most social media campaigns fail to reach their goals due to lack of consistent management. Poorly run campaigns will use a lot of your time, while only providing minimal results. Time is not a resource you can afford to waste.

Spend time optimizing your social media efforts up front based on your goals. Once you do, you will save time and get better results in terms of engagement, traffic, and conversions. Thankfully, there are hundreds of helpful social media marketing tools available to help you run your campaigns efficiently. Here are a few of my current favorites.

- **HOOTSUITE** – This is one of my favorite social media tools and one I use every day. Hootsuite allows you to manage several social media profiles at once and schedule posts to go out when you want. Social media relies on consistent content, but the reality is you may not be available to post every day. This tool allows you to pre-write and schedule posts to go out. Set up your weekly social media posts at one time and let it go. This is an incredibly useful and timesaving tool.

- **BUFFER** – Similar to Hootsuite, Buffer connects to all your social media channels and allows you to schedule posts. Some marketers prefer Buffer over Hootsuite, and Buffer does have some nice additional features. This makes posting regular content to social media quick and easy. Create posting schedules once and use your time on other projects.

- **COMMUN.IT** – This is a free service that helps you stay connected with your most important customers in one dashboard. The easy-to-use display lets you see who is posting what and whom you need to respond to. It helps you easily enhance relationships with your core customers.

- **IFTTT** – This is a more advanced plugin with lots of features that takes some getting used to, but can quickly improve your social media results. Best of all it's free to use! IFTTT stands for 'If This Then That' and creates a series of events based on your starting action. If this happens, then do that. For example, when you create a posting schedule in Buffer, IFTTT will automatically add it to your editorial calendar. These events are called *recipes*, and what I like most about this plugin is you can see other marketer's *recipes* or actions they're using. Huge time saver.

- **CYFE** – Strange name for a great tool. Cyfe combines analytics from multiple social media sources into one dashboard - quickly and easily monitors your results at a glance. You can monitor in real time how all of your social media channels are doing. Saves you time of jumping all over the internet by consolidating data into one screen.

- **AGORAPULSE** – Common questions that you'll ask yourself are "How well am I doing compared to my competitors? Are my social media campaigns as successful as theirs?" This used to be nearly impossible for small business owners to find out on a limited budget. Now you can get an answer. AgoraPulse offers detailed analysis of your competitor Facebook campaigns and how you compare to them. The simple reports show how you rank in fans, posts, interactions, and engagement. Their advanced stats go into even more detail about user interaction. AgoraPulse provides powerful information at an affordable price.

- **CROWDBOOSTER** – This is an impressive tool that monitors how well your posts do throughout the day, week, and month. It reports the number of impressions your posts received, at what time of day they happened, follower growth, and re-post numbers. Now you're able to see exactly when the best time to post content, is based on how active your followers are. Monitor when you'll get the highest response rate and track who's re-posting your comments the most. This is a great tool to use in conjunction with Hootsuite to maximize your social media effectiveness.

- **KINGSUMO HEADLINES** – This WordPress plugin allows you to easily A/B split test your headlines. Create multiple post titles in one screen, and Kingsumo will randomly show those headlines to visitors. You'll be able to quickly see which post is performing the best and optimize based on those results.

TIPS FROM THE EXPERTS

I've talked to the social media pros and here are their tips for running a successful media campaign:

- Determine your strategy first
  - o   Create **Brand Awareness**
  - o   Improve **Sales Conversion**
  - o   Increase **Customer Loyalty**

- Connect your social media campaign to a specific product page, opt-in or blog. This results in higher conversions than dropping them on your home page with no clear call-to-action. Use WordPress plugins to link social icons on your site to any social media channels you're using, and import any posts back to your website.

- Use photos that are visually interesting and intriguing. Social media has become incredibly visual, and posts with good photos see higher engagement rates. Tools such as Canva can help you create visually pleasing images to use across your channels. Post to Pinterest and Instagram regularly, and run a photo contest with followers.

- Post regularly and deliver relevant content. The more your audience hears from you, the more trust your brand. Social media is about building a relationship with your audience, not selling. Create regular conversations online to build a loyal community.

- Utilize the custom tabs on Facebook. Not enough businesses really use the four tabs below their cover photo. Maximize your site's features by providing additional information about your product in these tabs. Don't forget your call to action on those tabs and pages. Make any content you create on these pages shareable, so users can send it to their friends.

- Use #hashtags wisely and professionally. Do not get carried away and use more than two in any post. Build communities around actionable hashtags. Nike used #chooseyourwinter and #runfree as a way for people to easily share their adventures and posts.

- Offer followers incentives, but don't go fishing for likes. Contests or giveaways are a great idea to generate some buzz with your audience. Followers love free things. Don't simply ask them to like your page though. That should be done through quality content. Make your contest clear and have a defined call to action that meets your social goals. Twitter is a great place to test out social contests.

- **Post. Monitor. Analyze. Repeat.**

- Increase your engagement by narrowing your focus. It's easy to want to target everyone. This actually leads to lower engagement rates. Make your posts highly focused for a specific audience. When you see a post is doing well, boost it with a few dollars. This is a better strategy to reach potential customers. Select your highest performing posts each month and turn those into longer blog posts used on your site.

- Build your Google+ following. Google+ is not only a way of searching information, but it's also a social media site. The number of followers you have will impact your search rankings. Make sure to share your Google+ profile on other social media pages by placing a link to your profile on your website, forum profiles, social media accounts, blog accounts, and anywhere else it is allowed. Building your Google+ social media channel will help your SEO efforts as well.

Social media is fast paced and exciting. It offers businesses the opportunity to connect with customers instantly all over the world. If you build your social media campaign the right way and with the right expectations, you'll see enormous results. Social media is driven by content. Viewers are attracted by interesting and engaging information. Create content that is honest, informative, and unique. Be consistent with your branding, messages, and postings. The key to a successful social media campaign is not a mystery. It simply requires a commitment to innovation and interaction. Social media is constantly changing and offering new ways to connect with customers. While it can be overwhelming in the beginning, the rewards are waiting for you. Sign up for social media and take your business to the next level.

THE BACKCOUNTRY APPROACH

One of the most successful social media campaigns I've seen is from Backcountry.com. They are an online outdoor retailer located in Salt Lake City, Utah. They depend on a strong online community to further their web-based business. Backcountry.com has long been at the forefront of social media and has created sites that focus on consumer generated content. They use their Facebook page as an online forum for viewers to post photos, discuss gear, write reviews, and run promotions. Their Instagram feed thrives on users posted photos. By simply providing a space for users to share their information, Backcountry.com has created interactive social media with engaging, fresh, and relevant content. They have let their viewers determine the direction of their social media all while keeping consistent branding and messaging. A current look at their Facebook page shows almost 500,000 likes and over 17,000 people talking about them. By combining interactive social media with great customer service and unique sales strategies, Backcountry.com has risen towards the top of online retailers. Social media doesn't need to be complicated. Backcountry.com simply created an online forum for people to voice their opinions and share their lives. It is an excellent example of using social media the right way.

13

DON'T PAY FOR IT

How To Get It For Free

I hope you've got a clear picture now of what it takes to be an entrepreneur. You'll need to be extremely creative with your resources and bootstrap whenever possible. The key to making it past your first year is minimizing costs during the startup. I've talked about when to spend money and when to do it yourself. I've also detailed a plan to launch your company on limited resources. These cost-saving techniques can be the difference between making it over that hump or not making it past this month. Don't spend money on something when you can get it for free.

I am always impressed with how creative entrepreneurs can be. I'm sure that you'll be able to come up with unique solutions that benefit your company as well. You are going to face a lot of challenges, and your first instinct may be to spend money to get past it. I can't emphasize enough to always look for alternative solutions. Here are several unconventional methods

I've seen from entrepreneurs over the years. What unique approach can you come up with?

- **NETWORK, NETWORK, NETWORK** – One of the biggest benefits of college or business school is the networking. That guy who sat behind you in math class may be a whiz in analytics, or your friend who was the art major may be just the person you're looking for to design a logo. The people you meet can be extremely valuable in helping you later on. Luckily, there are lots of networking sites available to connect you with other people. Sites, like **LinkedIn.com** or **Meetup.com,** can be excellent resources for meeting people in your industry, field, or community. I suggest joining a networking site and get your name out there. People may also be looking for your services, so create a business page on LinkedIn. This is a great way to start partnerships. In addition, look for local networking events to attend. There are often entrepreneur socials and business luncheons that local Chamber of Commerce will host. Head over to those and meet other business owners in your community. The old saying of 'it's not what you know; it's who you know' is definitely true. Always look for networking opportunities and develop those relationships.

- **BOARD OF DIRECTORS** – Before you say I don't want to give up control in my company, hear me out. As a business owner, it may be wise to bring on a board of directors for additional expertise and experience. This can be extremely useful for you in adding resources and ideas to your company. Reach out to family, friends, established business owners, or professionals in your community to see if they'd be interested. As entrepreneurs, there is often an unwritten code to 'pay it back'.

Everyone has received help at some point, so when asked to help other startups, business owners are often happy to help. This board of directors doesn't need to hold any actual stock or investment in your company and can be thought of as a brain trust. Limit it to four or five people and ask for at least one year of service. Usually, board of directors meet once a month or quarterly to discuss how the company is doing, analyze strategies, and look at any new opportunities. Not only is this a great way to network, but it also expands your resources. All these people have networks of contacts as well. Best of all, an experienced board of directors can help you avoid mistakes or recover quicker when mistakes do happen. Diversity is good in business, so try to surround yourself with the best people possible.

- **CALL IN FAVORS** – Recruit friends to help you out. We've all heard of painting parties, where one friend invites you over to help paint a room and buys you pizza in return. Using your friends' help is a great way to get things done quickly. An 8-hour job will take all day by yourself. With two people it drops to four hours; with four people it drops to two hours; with eight people you just turned that all day project into one hour! Time is valuable when you have a full list of projects to accomplish. Calling in friends can be a lifesaver and perhaps even save you from having to pull that all-nighter. Keep the expectations reasonable, be considerate of their schedule, and reward them with something good, like pizza. You want to make certain they will come back and do it again.

- **NEGOTIATE** – The ancient art of trade is alive and well in the entrepreneur community. Explore trade options with people before you pay full price. Never be afraid to ask about alternative payments. Often people are willing to work out a deal. Negotiating is a skill you'll be able to use frequently, so practice it whenever possible. There are plenty of negotiation books and articles available for you to study up on. It is a skill that can save you thousands of dollars. Remember, be polite, be sincere, and when you get a price that works for you stick to it. They are exercising faith in you to make good on your promise.

Don't burn bridges. Failing to come through on your end
of the negotiation can cause negative feedback that is sure
to spread through their network. I call it sustainable
negotiations. Find a deal that works for both parties.

LET'S MAKE A DEAL

During the first year of Uproar Group Marketing, we decided to have
professional videos created to use on our website and post online. Through
connections, we found a highly recommended videographer willing to take
on our project. The only problem was his $2,500 price tag. We didn't have
those funds budgeted for media projects, but also knew we needed those
videos. So we started negotiating with him. After about an hour of
discussion, we had the price down to $500 and a promise to use him as our
exclusive video production company. That offer was great with me,
especially after I saw his final product. The videos turned out fantastic and
we saved $2,000. Always look for alternative solutions and never be afraid
to ask. You might be surprised what you find.

- **GUEST WRITING** – Since you are starting your own
  business, I trust that you are very knowledgeable in your
  field. A great way to gain exposure and reach your target
  market is to buy guest writing on blogs or publications.
  Choose several relative print or online publications that
  accept guest writers. These publications should be
  popular and well read by your target audience. Submit
  guest columns about topics you are experienced in.
  Become a regular contributor if possible. Customers will
  not only become familiar with you, but you will have an

opportunity to get your message in front of them. For example, if you've created a new type of vacuum that's better than others and you start writing articles about the advancement in vacuum technology to improve people's lives, that will get consumers to start thinking about the issue. Much like social media, do not treat this as a direct sales tool. It's simply a way to contribute relative content to the industry you're working in. Write engaging articles that outline a current problem and deliver a real solution that benefits your product. It's a great way to build customer recognition and credibility for your company.

- **FILL A NEED** – TV, radio, public relation, and media companies are always searching for new content. It's the product they deliver to their customers and the way they stay in business. Take advantage of this need by providing them new content. Contact local TV morning shows, radio programs, or podcasts to find out when they are doing a segment that relates to your company. Offer to provide their viewers something new and interesting. This comes back to quality content, because media outlets don't want boring material. Write a pitch that is relative and interesting to their target audience. Contact them to find out when you can be on. You may be surprised to find out how welcoming they can be. Media outlets are excited about newsworthy content, so create something worthwhile that fills their need. You might just get some great exposure for free.

- **SHARED INTERESTS** – Look for opportunities to partner with companies within your business channel. These are not direct competitors, but other companies that may share your same customers. Vacuum retailers share the same customer as carpet stores do. Athletic equipment suppliers share customers with nutrition drink makers. Look for companies that you share customers with, but are not in competition with.

Search out mutually beneficial relationships in your community. More recognized or established businesses can help build your brand recognition quickly. Keep the arrangements simple and flexible. Again, good negotiation skills are important to ensure you are get the most out of your efforts. Creating beneficial relationships can be a great way to get recognized, build your brand, and enter a new space quickly. Look for your opportunities.

14

MAXIMIZE YOUR OPERATIONS

How To Avoid Bottlenecks

It's an amazing feeling - your first sale. All of your efforts have paid off and someone actually bought your product. Then reality sets in and you feel a little unprepared. Relax; you're officially in business now, so it's time to work on your operations strategy. An operations strategy is your plan for seamlessly managing all the processes involved getting the product through manufacturing and to the customer. It details step-by-step the best way for you to produce and deliver your product. This plan will ensure your company runs smoothly at each step of the process. It covers everything from manufacturing to order taking, shipping, and customer retention. Your strategy will map out each step and give you a guide to run your business. Each company will have a different operations plan, but it is important that you develop your plan upfront. The last thing you want is not being able to deliver on your promise to the customer.

A good operations strategy will improve your efficiency and workflow.

As a startup, your goal is to operate as efficiently as possible. The plan we'll discuss is a simple model to get you started. It contains five categories or steps involved in the purchasing process. As your company grows, this will evolve and change to fit your operations. Let's develop your plan.

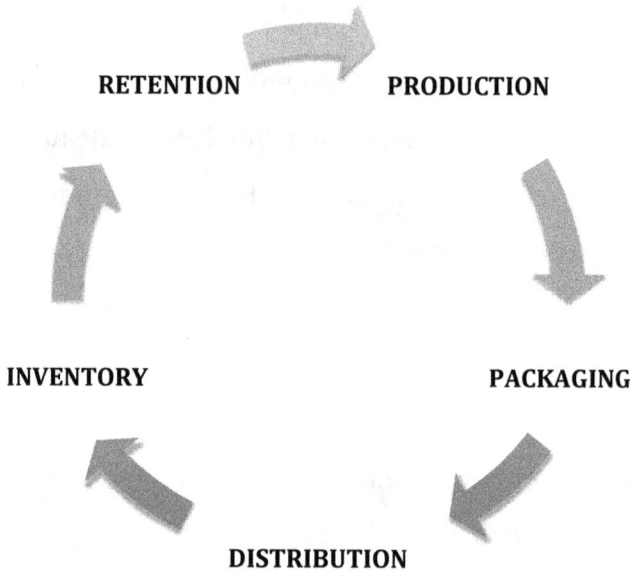

RETENTION   PRODUCTION

INVENTORY   PACKAGING

DISTRIBUTION

PRODUCTION

I assume by now you've produced your product, or at least are ready to start. Begin by detailing each step in the production process. Create a timeline of how your product is built, including materials, production time, and receiving time. As you map your production process, consider several important factors. What forces affect your manufacturing process? Are materials readily available or could there be a shortage? What forces could cause that to change?

Cement is a great example of this. As world economies grow, especially China, infrastructures are expanding at record pace. The demand for cement is incredibly high right now creating a shortage. New homebuilders in the United States saw prices of cement skyrocket last year as a result. The higher costs ate into their margins and impacted their pricing strategy.

Examine each step of your production process and create a 'what if' scenario. What if my shipping company goes out of business? What if there is a labor strike? Does it have to pass through customs? Understand how these factors could impact your production and create back-up plans for each step of the process. Also, understand order times. This is the time it takes from the time you place the order to when you receive the product. Does that fluctuate based on quantity or time of year? You'll use this information to forecast future orders. We'll dive into this shortly, but starting out you do not want to carry a lot of inventory. You don't have the space or capital to hold a large inventory. Understanding the order time is essential for ensuring you are stocked with the right products and the customer receives their purchase on time.

PACKAGING

How does your packaging look at this point? Remember, packaging is the first thing consumers' see and must represent your branding. It plays an important role in your product's success. Your packaging should be interesting, clear, uncluttered, and professional looking. Did you run A/B testing on it and what were the results? Did it resonate well with the test group? You want to make sure that your packaging is customer ready.

Next, you want to focus on the cost, performance, security, safety, and sustainability of your packaging. What are the requirements your packaging must meet? Government regulations can have a large impact on package requirements. It's important to weigh each of these factors and understand how they can affect you. If you make a food product for instance, your package requirements are fairly strict. How readily available is the packaging and does it require a special order or longer amount of time to receive? Also, look for ways to improve your design while cutting costs. Packaging can be expensive and decrease your margins. Before you go out and order several thousand boxes, make sure you've done your research and are making the best decisions.

DISTRIBUTION

I'm going to keep this one simple. If you are an online business, then you'll need to set up an efficient shipping process. Chances are you do not have a fully staffed warehouse to take care of this for you. Most likely you'll be doing the fulfillment and shipping right out of your own home. Thankfully, picking a reliable distribution channel is fairly simple. There are several established shipping companies in the United States like UPS, FedEx, and USPS, that can take care of all your needs. Get price quotes from each of them to see which one will be the best for you. Each of them has great small business solutions to help you and most of them will even provide you with free shipping supplies. If you're shipping a lot of products each day, then it is worthwhile setting up a corporate account. I can tell you that standing in line waiting to drop off a package is frustrating and wastes valuable time. Invest in a thermal label printer, so you can preprint labels at home and simply drop them off or have them picked up. It's much quicker and will save you time. Don't forget to brand the outside of your box with your name or tagline.

If you're selling through a storefront location, then you need to make sure your product arrives on time. Again, pick the best company that meets your needs and provides the best price. Get quotes from them on monthly delivery costs, and ensure there is a smooth pickup process at the manufacturer. If your products are coming from outside the United States, then they will have to clear customs. This requires special paperwork to be filled out before shipping. It's a good idea to call your local customs office to find out more information ahead of time.

In addition, communicate with the manufacturer about any special requirements or paperwork to ensure they are aware of it.

For large shipments, it is worthwhile to hire a customs broker. They take care of all the paperwork and make certain your delivery clears customs without any problems. I can tell you first hand that having a shipment stuck in customs can take weeks to resolve and is very frustrating. All the time customers are waiting. Examine your delivery process and the distribution channel from start to finish. Identify any challenges that could hold up your shipment and resolve them.

COMPANY	PHONE NUMBER	SMALL BUSINESS WEBSITE
US POSTAL SERVICE	800-222-1811	www.usps.com/business/ business-solutions.htm
UPS	800-742-5877	www.ups.com/smallbiz
FEDERAL EXPRESS	800-463-3339	www.fedex.com/us/small-business/

INVENTORY

Managing your inventory is a challenging process. Few of us have experience with managing inventory or understanding where the problems lie. Even fewer of us can actually create inventory plans to ensure our operations run smoothly. Yet it is incredibly vital to understand how inventory works in order to manage it effectively. In business school, there is an entire semester spent on managing processes. It's all about finding the bottlenecks in your process, solving them, and maximizing production flow. I'll be the first to admit this can be confusing information, and I'm going to throw a few math formulas at you. Don't run away and ignore this. It's important to learn. I'll simplify the process and make it easy to understand. Soon you'll be able to balance production and inventory like a pro. Let's get started.

Managing processes is a strategy that effectively coordinates inputs and outputs - when do materials arrive at the factory, how long does it take to assemble the product, what's the shipping time from the factory to your location, how fast are you selling the product, and how much inventory are you holding as a result? It is any process that takes inputs and turns them into outputs. Visualize the whole process like this.

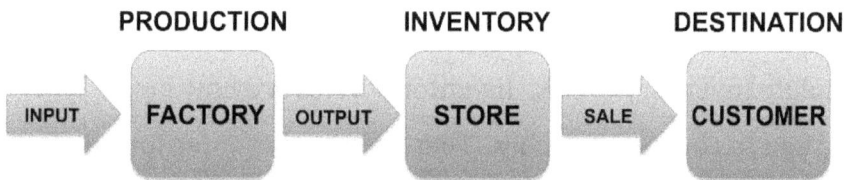

PRODUCTION	INVENTORY	DESTINATION
INPUT → FACTORY → OUTPUT	STORE	SALE → CUSTOMER

The process overview is relatively simply. Tangible goods flow in and out of the market. Your challenge is to make that process as smooth and efficient as possible. Large companies spend millions of dollars managing their processes and are always looking for ways to improve it. I previously stated that one advantage of small businesses is you are able to react quicker to changing market trends. You can take advantage of spikes in demand faster than larger companies can. However, what if you have to wait six months to get your product delivered? You may miss out on the market trend all together. Without efficient processes, you create delays in your reaction and delivery time. Customers are forced to wait for your product and in that time they're searching for substitute.

When you go to the grocery store for orange juice and they're out of it, do you wait two weeks for them to restock it? No, you go to another grocery store and buy it. Customers want their products right away after the purchase. If you ask them to wait, you risk losing that customer all together. That's why this concept is so valuable, because your revenue depends on it. Once again, I've stripped it down to make it easier and give you the information that you need to know.

There are a few simple formulas called *Little's Law* that calculate inventory cycles. Inventory cycles are how long it will take you to run out of supply. These are fairly simple formulas with three variables. I've written the same formula below for each variable:

TIME = INVENTORY / RATE
RATE = INVENTORY / TIME
INVENTORY = RATE x TIME

These three formulas measure the flow of product and cycle times. Time is simply the amount of time before your inventory is depleted. Rate is how quickly you go through your inventory. And inventory is how much product you currently have stocked. Let's look at a quick example of a fast food restaurant.

Hamburger Hut sells 5,000 hamburgers per week. Each hamburger patty is 1 lb of meat. They currently have 2,500 lbs of hamburger meat in their refrigerators. What is the inventory cycle time and when will they run out of hamburger meat?

Start by plugging in your information. Rate = 5,000 lbs of hamburger meat per week. Inventory = 2,500 lbs of hamburger meat. We need to figure out the time. Time = Inventory / Rate or 2,500 / 5,000 = 0.5 weeks. This means that the Hamburger Hut will run out of inventory in 0.5 weeks or 3.5 days. The cycle time is 1/Time. This means the inventory cycle is 1/.5 = 2 or twice per week.

From a few simple calculations we now know that they'll run out of inventory in 3.5 days and they go through their inventory (cycle time) twice per week. It would be wise of the owner to set up meat delivery every 3 days.

Let's try another example focused on customer service. You can use these formulas to see how long customers wait and how long they spend in your store.

Your deli processes 150 customers per day. Assume that you are open for 10 hours each day. On average, there are 10 people in the deli either waiting to place their order, waiting for food, or eating. How long does the average customer spend in your deli?

We know that Rate = 150 customers per day. Inventory = 10 customers. We need to figure out time. Time = Inventory / Rate or 10/150 = 0.0667 days. That number doesn't mean much, so let's convert it from days to minutes. Your deli is open 10 hours per day, so we multiply 0.0667 x 10 hours = 0.667 hours x 60 minutes = 40 minutes. The average customer spends 40 minutes in your restaurant.

This is great information to know. It allows you to tailor your marketing and customer service more effectively. If your customers are businessmen and women on a one-hour lunch break, this fits their schedule. What if your average time was 70 minutes? Do you think you'd get a lunch crowd? It also allows you to look for ways to speed the process up. If you can improve that average time to 30 minutes, you may be able to get more customers through your deli for a higher rate.

Let's do one more about cash flow. You can use these same equations to see how much money you have tied up in accounts receivable. As a small business, every dollar counts. These funds could be essential to your strategy and really impact your plan, if they are tied up in receivables.

Your cellphone company sells $300,000 worth of cell equipment per year. Unfortunately, you have some people who do not pay their bills. Your average time to send a customer to collections and get payment is 10 weeks. Let's assume that there are 50 business weeks in the year. What is your average accounts receivable amount?

For this example, we know the Rate = $300,000 per year. We also know the time is 10 weeks. What we need to figure out is the Inventory. Remember Inventory = Rate x Time. First, we need to do a quick conversion. You see the rate is per year and the time is in weeks. We need to convert the rate into weeks. So we divide $300,000 / 50 weeks per year = $6,000 per week. Now we're ready to plug in the numbers. Inventory = $6,000 x 10 weeks = $60,000.

You currently have $60,000 tied up in collection accounts. Think of what else you could be using those funds for. As the business owner, it would be wise to look for better collection *agencies to bring that time down. Even if you cut that from 10 weeks to 5 weeks collection time that decreases your receivables from $60,000 to $30,000. You just earned yourself an extra $30,000 in revenue by improving the process.*

Do you see how a few simple formulas can dramatically improve your revenue or customer experience? Spend the time to analyze your business and map out the process. Calculate times, rates, and inventories for your current processes. Ask yourself if those are working or if you need to improve them? Now we're going to get a little more in depth into this process. We're going to revisit your deli, but this time we're going to map the customer flow as they move through the deli. Our goal is to identify any bottlenecks. Bottlenecks are problem areas where the process slows down. Something causes the flow to decrease, creating a delay down the line. Bottlenecks are extremely common in business. Your goal is look to for yours. I guarantee you have a bottleneck somewhere in your processes. See if you can find it and fix it.

FIND THE BOTTLENECK

Your deli is growing. Customers enter your deli at a rate of 60 people per hour. You have two main stations for people to get their food. One for sandwiches and one for soups and salads. You also have a drink machine next to each station and a coffee machine by the register. There is one cash register all customers pay at after selecting their food. For simplicity sake, let's assume that customers are either getting a sandwich or soup/salad, but not both. Customers have three paths to go through your deli. Path 1: they go to get their sandwich and drink, then pay. Path 2: they get a soup/salad and a drink, then pay. Path 3: they go straight to get a coffee and pay. You stand at the door for an hour and take note on where people go. You notice that 18 people go to get sandwiches, 36 people get soup or a salad, and 6 people go straight to just get their coffee. You also notice that, on average, 2 people are waiting at the sandwich station and 1 to get their drink. 5 people are waiting at the soup/salad station with 0 people waiting for a drink, and 0 people also are waiting to get coffee. When people have everything they need picked out, they head to pay. The average wait time at the register is 6 minutes. How long does it take people to get their food and sit down? What is the average time it takes people to get their food?

This may seem like a really complicated problem, but in actuality it's pretty simple. It just requires some drawing and a table. Grab some paper and see if you can map out the path people take through your deli. Draw the three different paths they can take. It will look something like this:

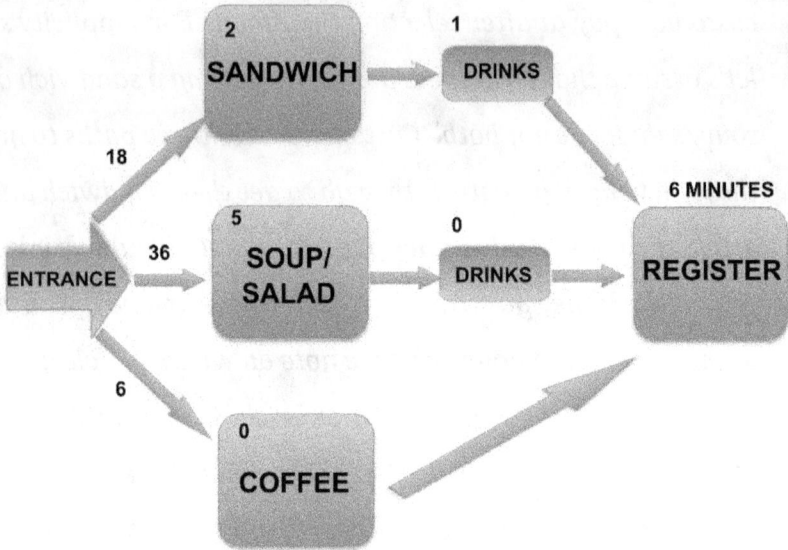

This shows the three different paths customers take when they enter your deli. It also has the number of people that go to each station along with how many are waiting. Out of the 60 people per hour, 18 people go to the sandwich station, 2 are waiting there, and 1 is waiting for a drink. 36 people go to the soup/salad station where 5 people are waiting but none for drinks. 6 people go straight for coffee and, again, nobody is waiting. They eventually all make their way to the register where it takes an average of 6 minutes to checkout. You just condensed that confusing problem down to a simple and manageable flow chart. It's easy to see how customers move through your deli. Now it's time to calculate how long it takes customers to move through each path and get their food.

We'll make a table using the Time, Inventory, and Rate variables to determine how long each path takes. The rate is the number of people going to each station per hour. The inventory is how many people are waiting at those stations. And the time is how long it takes for each person to travel through the stations. I've added an additional column for total time, because after each person gets their food they must wait 6 minutes to checkout. We need to add this time into the total time. You'll have a time to get food and a total time to actually sit down and eat. Let's plug in our numbers right from the flow chart above.

STATION	RATE	INVENTORY	TIME	TOTAL TIME
SANDWICH	18	2+1 = 3	3/18 = .167 hr = 10 minutes	16 minutes
SOUP/SALAD	36	5+0 = 5	5/36 = .138 hr = 8.3 minutes	14.3 minutes
COFFEE	6	0	0/6 = 0 hr = 0 minutes	6 minutes

*For each one, we know the Rate and Inventory. Time =
Inventory / Rate. Use that to calculate your Time. The number
you get is in hours, so it will be a small decimal. Multiply by 60
to convert that number to minutes. For the total, time we
simply add the time at each station with the 6 minutes at the
register.*

*With a few easy steps, you just mapped out your flow chart and
the time it takes for each person to get their food. It takes 16
minutes for a sandwich, 14.3 minutes for soup/salad, and 6
minutes for coffee. Even though twice the number people of
went for a soup/salad and had more people waiting at that
station, their total wait time was less than the people with
sandwiches. How do you adjust your processes or marketing
based on this information?*

*Can you identify the bottleneck? Where is the process moving
at its slowest point? What does that mean for business? Get
used to thinking about what these numbers actually mean in
terms of revenue. What is your highest margin product? In
this example, let's say sandwiches have the highest margin and
make you the most money. Right now, fewer people get
sandwiches and wait longer. To increase your revenue, you
need to get more people through the sandwich line. This means
speeding up the process. Invest in more sandwich makers or*

simplify the process. Also, in case you didn't already identify it, the cash register is your bottleneck. It accounts for 38% of Path 1's wait, 42% of Path 2's wait, and 100% of Path 3's wait. You'd be smart to get another register and come up with a way that people only getting coffee don't need to wait at all.

Do you see how avoiding bottlenecks and effectively managing your processes can have a huge impact on your revenue? Sit down and develop simple flow charts like these for your processes. Create charts for both manufacturing and sales. You need to clearly see where the bottlenecks are in each process. Work on improving those and you'll see your bottom line improve along with it.

There is one last formula that will come in handy as you develop your processes. It calculates the best order size and how long that inventory will last. As you look for ways to cut costs, determining the ideal order size will be very useful. You don't want to order too much at once, but you also don't want to sell out too quickly and be left without any inventory. In business school, they call this the economic order quantity or EOQ.

$$EOQ = \sqrt{(2RS/H)}$$

EOQ represents the ideal order size or quantity for your business. R is the rate. This is the demand or annual sales volume. S is the order cost - how much the product costs to buy or manufacture. Finally, H is the holding cost. This is the amount it costs you to keep it in your inventory. For instance, if your warehouse costs $10,000 per year and you have 1,000 units in inventory, then your holding cost is $10,000/1,000 = $10 per unit per year. Let's work through an example of finding the ideal order size (EOQ).

You decided to start a satellite TV company and need to determine the ideal order size for your satellite dishes. You estimate that you will sell 1,000 dishes in your first year. The dishes cost you $30 to buy and the carrying cost per dish is $50 each year.

What is your ideal order size? How long will that order last before having to reorder?

As before, let's start plugging in the information. Rate (R)= 1,000. Holding Cost (H) = $50. Order Cost (S) = $30. So the EOQ = $\sqrt{(2*1000*30)}/50$. EOQ = 34.64 or 35 if we round up. This means the ideal order size is 35 satellite dishes. Next, let's figure out how long that order will last you.

Order frequency is simply O=EOQ/R. O is our inventory cycle time and how long our inventory will last. We just calculated EOQ, which is our ideal order size. And R is our Rate. Plug in the numbers to get O=35/1000 or 0.035 years. Let's convert that into a more meaningful number in days. Simply multiply by 365 days/year so 0.035 x 365 = 12.77 days.

In this example you just figured out that in order to minimize your inventory costs, it is best to order 35 satellite dishes at a time and you'll be re-ordering every 12 days. This allows you to now plan storage space, setup the best delivery times, and save money on shipping. Congratulations! You just found the best EOQ and are saving money over your competitor who doesn't know how to calculate this!

Creating a good strategy, and managing your processes effectively will help to balance your inventory and lower your costs. You never want to have too much or too little inventory. It is a challenge to find just the right balance of inventory amount. Order too much and you will incur huge holding costs, not to mention if the product has any type of expiration on it. Then you risk not being able to sell it all in time. On the other hand, order too little and you won't have enough to meet the demand for it. If you run out, you run the risk that customers will simply go elsewhere. Finding the right inventory balance is key for managing your processes effectively. Using this information and these examples, you should be able to calculate your own inventory cycle times. Then you'll be able to come up with an order schedule that makes sense and satisfies demand. That is the secret to managing processes and higher revenues.

CUSTOMER RETENTION

Finally, the last step in your operations plan is customer retention. This step is all about the customer and providing great service. Repeat after me "I'm not right." A good customer service strategy should be designed *for* the customer to meet *their* needs and resolve their problems. Customer service is part of the foundation for every great company. It is something you should develop early, always work on improving, and place at the forefront of your operations strategy. Why should you care about customer service? I have three reasons that should make you develop a phenomenal customer service policy.

The first reason you should care about customer service is your company's image. Companies with great customer service stand out, compared to those companies that don't. Customer service can add to your branding and company's image. Poor customer service can just as easily detract from it. Think about a bad customer service experience you had. How many people did you tell about it? How many people do you think they have told about it? One bad review can be more powerful than ten good reviews. Bad reviews find a way of grabbing people's attention and sticking out. I've found myself focusing on bad reviews when researching products. I can be browsing through a dozens of five star ratings and it's always the one-star rating that stands out. I tend to read those reviews more and tell myself I don't want that to happen to me. Beware of bad ratings and understand the impact they can have. Information spreads quickly in this day and age, thanks to social media. Trust me, you'd much rather have good publicity starting out than bad publicity. You may think that returns will cost you money, but a good customer service policy will make you more in the long run.

THE NO PROBLEM APPROACH

Good customer service can also increase consumer confidence and influence them to buy from you versus an unknown outlet. Backcountry.com has done an excellent job with the customer service and return policies. They make the return process simple, easy, and hassle free. My personal experience has always been that they will return any item for exchange or refund without question. If it's not the right size or not exactly what I wanted, I don't have to worry about sending it back. It's no problem. Their customer service policy has actually created more confidence in the buying experience, because I know that I don't have to worry about anything. Not only do I recommend that other people purchase from them, but I am now willing to spend a little more on a product to purchase it through them as well. It's worth it for me to spend a few more dollars for the assurance of good customer service. For Backcountry.com a good customer service policy has helped increase their bottom line.

The second reason you should care about good customer service is the price of customers. Earning new customers is more expensive than retaining current customers. In some situations, those, costs can be 10:1 higher for new customers. It benefits your bottom line to keep your existing customer happy. You already have their contact information and know they are interested in your product. Your marketing is done. With new customers, you have to spend money to go out and find them. By ignoring existing customers, you are throwing money away. Create a customer service policy that is focused on the customer. Build a policy that makes them happy. Remember, this isn't about you; it's about the customer. Give them what they want within reason. Combine this strategy with a good CRM system (Customer Relationship Management) that we talked about in Chapter 9. Keep in touch with your existing customers, send them promotions, and give them a great experience to keep them coming back.

The third reason for having excellent customer service is for your own internal culture. You need to create a culture that is focused on taking care of the customer and their needs. Having a clear policy that benefits your customer sends a message to employees and partners that you value their business. This adds to a healthy culture when employees care about the customer. Culture is catchy. Good examples can spread through your company just like bad examples do. You need to set the expectation right up front that your main focus is the customer. This will help to improve your own internal culture.

That's it. There is your operations plan. Integrate and follow through on each of those five steps. You'll see an improvement in ordering, delivery, and customer satisfaction. You'll also see an improvement on your bottom line. Get used to thinking about each of your decisions in terms of revenue. How will my decisions affect my profit? Where am I able to improve my processes? Think about your customer's experience. Focus on three things: product quality, delivery time, and customer service. Each of these relies on how well you manage the processes from start to finish. I've given you enough information to get started. These are easy to follow steps that can give you a competitive advantage over your competition and dramatically improve your bottom line.

THAT'S A STUPID DECISION

A few weeks ago, my cellphone completely died, so I called my phone company to explore getting a new one. It turns out that I'd had my phone for one year and two weeks from my date of purchase when it died. They would only cover phones within one year of purchase. The sales rep at this very large and national phone company refused to help me out replacing my phone at a reasonable price. The only solution he offered was a $75 discount on buying a new phone. With the cost of phones today, I still was looking at paying over $200 plus a brand new two-year contract. This solution wasn't what I wanted but was willing to negotiate. Unfortunately, he was not and only offered the one solution. It became extremely frustrating. Getting nowhere, I requested to speak with his supervisor, hoping for a better resolution. Again, I received the same offer and refusal to do anything else. At this point, I became so frustrated that I asked the supervisor how much it would cost to cancel my service and break my contract. I could get a free phone switching to another carrier. He told me $250. I replied, "It's worth it to pay $250 and not have to deal with this poor customer service." Faced with losing a customer his response was, "You'd rather pay $250 to leave than pay $200 for a new phone? Well that's a stupid decision." Both representatives I spoke with that evening refused to solve the problem, treat me like a valued customer after five years with them, and shared the same attitude. Poor customer service is infectious. It spreads throughout your company and will hurt your revenue. Now, I happily tell my story to anyone in hopes of steering them away from this company. I'm also enjoying my new phone that I got for free.

15

FINDING INVESTORS

Money Costs Too Much

Y ou've reached the point that you are ready to expand. Sales are increasing and it is time to grow. Just one problem...your savings is empty. **STOP** right there! Before you go any further, make sure that you are ready to bring on an investor. Every entrepreneur will face this decision. The reality is: expansion requires capital. Often we simply do not have that much money just lying around. When you don't have enough money, you need to go look for more. Where you find the new capital and the terms you negotiate for it are vital to your success. Everything is at stake when you take on investors. Take on too much new capital and you may lose your controlling share or not be able to afford the payments. Take on too little and it may not get you to your goal. Then you've given away a piece of your company and are still in need of more capital. In addition, your relationship with the investor is critical. You may be dealing with that person every day. Finding the right investor at the right price is a difficult challenge. There is plenty of money out there chasing a few good ideas. The problem is not finding money. The challenge is to get the most for it. You need to know where to look and how to create leverage. In this chapter, we'll teach you how to find investors.

FIND MR. RIGHT

The biggest mistake entrepreneurs make is settling too quickly on an offer. They don't feel as if they can be choosy or negotiate a better deal, less they risk losing the money all together. I'm here to tell you that, if you have a solid enough company to receive one offer, then others will come. First and foremost, wait for the right opportunity. Did you marry the very person you kissed? If you did, then congratulations. If not and you're like the rest of us, then you know how looking around can improve your chance of compatibility and happiness. Finding capital is no different. Don't rush into taking the first offer. Make sure it's the right one for you and only then decide if you go for it.

When evaluating a potential investor, look at your personal relationship. How well do you get along together and what capacity will you be working together? A silent partner will be much more hands-off than an investor who wants to be involved in the day-to-day operations. Examine how well you work together, because you may be working closely with that person for years. If you can't stand the person, it's probably not a good idea to have them financially vested in your company. Also, look for investors that have your best interests in mind. Stay away from investors that seem selfish, only concerned with their position, or may be invested with a competitor. You want someone who is pulling for you and determined to see you succeed. Measure investors on their overall attitude and positivity. Do they help the relationship or tear it down? Are they team players? We've mentioned that you do not want to willingly bring in negative attitudes into your culture. Find investors that add to the experience. Make sure you've got a good personal relationship with any potential investor.

Next, what value do they bring to the table? What industry experience or expertise? Is it solely a financial contribution or are they bringing other tangible assets? Have they worked in your industry before and what were the results? Often, investors will bring their networks and sales channels along with them. Think about how useful that would be to instantly gain new sales channels and contacts. Select an investor that brings significant value to your company beyond the money. Don't be afraid to ask for references from the investors. Contact the previous companies they've worked with and see what they think of them. What value did the investor bring them? Was it worthwhile and how does the company feel about their decision now? Get outside opinions about what you're getting yourself into.

Perform a background check on any potential investor. I'm not necessarily referring to a credit check, but fully research any investor you decide to work with. Where is their money coming from, what are their current investments, how are those companies doing, what are their personal investments, and do they have any bankruptcies or glaring negative marks? Look them up on social media to learn more about them personally. Create an accurate picture of who this person is and their success rate of investing. When you speak with other companies they've invested in, try to get information about their term sheet. What terms were they offered compared to yours? If it's a better offer, why is that? Get to know as much background information as you legally can. So, now you know what to look for. Let's discuss where to find investors.

Investors are also looking for Mr. Right. They often see dozens of applicants each week in search of the best opportunity. Just as you're researching investors expect the same from them. They will look into your background and closely analyze who you are. Be prepared to provide full disclosure not only on the company but also on you. If you have any issues, it's best to disclose those upfront. Investors measure your character and strength as well. It's natural that you want to present your best side and make a great impression. Be professional about your company and life, but also be ready to discuss details when they ask. An honest conversation upfront will help to create confidence with the investor.

TURN OVER EVERY ROCK

There is no shortage of money chasing good ideas. So where do you find capital? Here are the most common types of investors:

FAMILY AND FRIENDS - Family and friends are often already emotionally invested in your company and can be a good source of capital. Take advantage of the relationships you have. Reach out to people in your life. Politely and professionally, ask personal acquaintances if they'd be interested in investing financially. Personal investors can be easy to access, but carry the same risks. Treat them like any other investor. Provide an accurate assessment of your company, plans, goals, strategies, and challenges. Openly discuss how you plan to spend the new capital and what you hope to accomplish. Don't expect them to give you the money for free either. Discuss fair terms that other investors would ask for. If they agree, sign a contract or partnership agreement outlining the details. This agreement should include size of the investment, rate of return, ownership arrangements, and any other details involving the company.

PROS: You have an established relationship with them. They are, hopefully, already supportive of your venture.
CONS: Personal relationships are at risk, if the investment fails. Line between friendship and investor can be easily blurred. Difficult to maintain a professional relationship.

VENTURE CAPITALISTS - Venture Capitalists (or VCs) are simply other companies looking to invest their money in a new emerging business. They invest new capital into these businesses during various stages of their operations. They typically look for startup companies with a new or unique technology, such as biotechnology, IT, or software, that also have a high growth potential. They look for very large margins and extremely large market size. VCs invest in several companies at once, hoping 1 or 2 of them will reach their potential and payoff. VC's can have minimum investment limits as well, based on their business model. If a VC has a $1 million minimum investment that indicates the size and scope of companies, they're looking at. In return for their investment, VCs ask for equity in your company. Don't be surprise to find that the equity amount requested is quite high. VCs want to maximize their investment, so are after the highest share they can get. Generally, in order to qualify for VC's investment, you need to show a history of sales and returns. Therefore, rarely will brand new companies in their initial funding stage receive an investment from a VC. This is good, because as we've discussed you do not want to give away equity too early. The more your company is worth, the less equity you must give away for that investment. VCs can be notorious for their aggressive negotiations. Weigh your options carefully, and fully research these types of investments, before going after VC funding.

PROS: VCs are typically very experienced and have established sales channels. You can gain valuable resources picking the right VC. They generally invest enough money based on a long term strategy funding you through your growth.

CONS: VCs ask for a large amount of equity in return for their investment. The terms of their investment often impact the entire structure of the company. It's possible to lose controlling share of your company. VC's can often take months to decide and provide funds.

ANGEL INVESTORS - Angel Investors are similar to VCs, but on a smaller scale. Angel Investors are typically an individual or small investment company searching for unconventional business ideas to fund. They are often after niche ideas that other investors may pass over or have difficulty investing in. Angel Investors may also have more flexible investment requirements and are able to base their decisions on intangibles. Angel Investors can invest anywhere from a few thousand to a few hundred thousand dollars. This works well for the majority of startups that simply don't require a million-dollar investment. In return for their funding, Angel Investors may ask for a return on investment, monthly payments, an equity share, or a combination of all three. While Angel Investors are typically more willing to negotiate on the terms than VCs, still make certain to perform your due

diligence. Find out what terms they have offered other
businesses for funding.

PROS: Smaller funding amounts better suited for your needs;
tend to fund ideas that fall outside VC or bank loan requirements;
greater flexibility with their investments and terms.

CONS: Still may require a large equity share in return for their
investment. Angel Investors can also take months to pick an
investment and provide funding.

PEER-TO-PEER LENDING – Peer-to-Peer lending is where a group
of investors, either companies or individuals, get together to fund
a small business. This market is exploding, with many different
options to explore. This type of lending is typically done online.
Business owners create an online profile for potential investors to
review. Investors can either donate a portion or fund the entire
amount required. The business owner negotiates the terms and
payment rate the investor will receive. Some peer-to-peer
lending outlets actually have the investors bid on the business
idea.   Kickstarter.com is a very popular peer to peer investment
site for startups, although there are many others you can easily
find online. Peer-to-peer lending sites typically do not have as
strict of requirements from investors, making it easier for
startups to receive funding. These are worth exploring for any
funding needs you may have.

PROS: Owners have more control over setting investment terms; can be a faster process to receive funds; do not have to give up an equity share if you don't want to; better suited for small amounts under $100,000.

CONS: Investors may not have any experience or value to contribute to your company. Instead of having one VC or Angel Investor, you may have many investors to work with.

BANKS - Banks provide businesses Small Business Administration (SBA) Loans or small business loans. SBA is a United States government-backed business loan program. Bank funding is a more conservative approach to funding. SBA loans have similar steps and requirements to getting a home or car loan. Business owners are required to complete paperwork, detailing their finances and business history. Banks run a background check and underwriters either approve or deny the loan. SBA loans do not require equity in return, but instead have a set interest rate with monthly payments to repay the loan. SBA loans can often have strict requirements and be a lengthy process, but they come with a lower amount of risk than other investment types.

PROS: Your business does not have to give up any equity in return for investment; government backed program; SBA loans have set terms and payment amounts that you can plan for; often more stable than VC or Angel investments.

CONS: You must show significant and favorable sales to underwriters; stricter requirements than other investment types.

INVESTMENT TYPE	INFORMATION SOURCE
PERSONAL RELATIONSHIPS	Friends, family, coworkers, professional network
VENTURE CAPITALIST (VC)	www.findventure.com www.entrepreneur.com/vc100 www.nvca.org
ANGEL INVESTORS	https://angel.co/ www.angelcapitalassociation.org/ www.mycapital.com/index.php
PEER TO PEER	www.kickstarter.com www.indiegogo.com www.gofundme.com
BANK LOANS	www.sba.gov www.sba.gov/category/lender-navigation/search-sba-lenders

These are the five most common sources of investment, but they aren't the only ones. If there is one message you take from this book, it's to be creative. Look for investment opportunities anywhere you can find them. Network with other entrepreneurs you've met or go after government grants. Many cities will have small business loan funds they are required to use each year. Research what type of small business support your community has. Pick the best type of investor for your needs. You are bringing this investor into your company, so make smart decisions. It's easy to be blinded by the dollar signs and not consider what you're really giving up. This is your future, so it's important to set it up the right way. Only accept offers that you are comfortable with. You may also need future rounds of investments, so consider if this first deal leaves you in a good position for those. There are lots of important decisions to be made when bringing on an investor. Choose one you have a good relationship with and one that will provide you the best chance at success. Once you have made those decisions, then you're ready to go after the money.

16

THE SECRET OF RAISING CAPITAL

How To Perfect Your Pitch

In my opinion, most entrepreneurs fail to get capital, not because their business idea is bad, but because their investor pitch is awful. I have sat through many investment presentations that are just terrible. They fail to effectively communicate their value or engage the audience. I have also been on the other end and, when first starting out, gave some poor investor pitches myself. As a result, I've been turned down for capital as well. There is an art and style to a good investor presentation. I'll give you some simple guidelines to make an effective presentation and separate yourself from the competition. Investors can sit through dozens of pitches each week. No doubt it is easy to get lost in the cluster of average small business owners. This information will help you stand out, grab their attention, and make a better pitch. Here are the secrets to a good investor presentation that I've learned over the years:

First, select the type of investor you are going after. Is it a VC, Angel Investor, Peer-to-Peer, SBA loan, or personal investment? Knowing your audience will determine how you put the pitch together. Next, contact them to set up a meeting time and get any application material you will need to fill out. Most investors will have an application to fill out. A fee of $25-$50 is fairly standard, but be careful if they ask for more. If you are applying for an Angel or VC, getting an appointment may be a little tricky. VCs usually accept appointments by-invitation-only and are scheduled for months out. If you contact a VC, don't be surprised if you don't hear back from them right away. Applying to a VC or Angel Investor takes persistence. This is where your networking becomes useful. Find people who know someone on that VC's board and work on a meeting that way. When you are building up your network, keep track of people you meet who are connected to VCs or Angel Investors. Those contacts can come in handy later on. Schedule your presentation time and complete any required paperwork.

Investors may require that you send them a Business Plan to review with your application. A Business Plan is simply a more in-depth Sales & Marketing plan that you have already put together. The next chapter is all about writing an effective Business Plan for investors, so if they request one you'll know exactly what they are looking for. Lengthy Business Plans between 30 and 40 pages long used to be a standard request from investors. We've seen that change slightly and Business Plans are used more as a formality now. I believe a 10 to 15-page plan is more effective for your presentation and cuts out much of the 'fluff' information. The Sales & Marketing plans you have already written are about 10 pages, so your Business Plan will just build upon those. Anything you present to investors should be on topic, get to the point quickly, and only provide relevant information. Short, sweet, and hard hitting is my philosophy. Give the investors what they need to know right up front. Once you have written an effective Business Plan, send it over for the investor to review ahead of time.

The secret to a good investor presentation is to get straight to the important information. Make it simple, easy to understand, and informative. You want them to remember three things: **the problem, the solution,** and **how you're going to make money**. That's it. If at the end of your presentation the investors either don't know those three things or they don't remember them, then you didn't prepare an effective pitch. Keep that principle in mind when you create your presentation. Now, let's start building your winning pitch.

ELEVATOR PITCH

No Science Allowed

Start the presentation to the investors with your elevator pitch. An elevator pitch is a short 20 to 30-second-long conversation that is simple and memorable. It is not a sales pitch! An elevator pitch tells the audience exactly what you do in 30 seconds. It engages them, peaks their curiosity, and invites them in for more. It answers the *what, how,* and *why* of your product. Think of it as the movie trailer for a blockbuster film. It provides a preview of the film, highlights the most interesting scenes, and makes the viewer anxious to see it. This is exactly what you want to do at the start of your presentation. You want to hook the audience with an interesting and exciting overview. A good elevator pitch creates a buzz and grabs them right from the start.

To write an effective elevator pitch, leave out the science, numbers, and technology behind your product. Nothing makes eyes glaze over faster than a bunch of technical jargon, and you don't want to lose your audience right from the start. Leave the industry terms and awesome technical details out of it. Instead focus on the benefits. Make your pitch 30 seconds of engaging, clear, concise, simple, and to-the-point information.

Describe the problem your product addresses, the solution your product delivers, and the value consumers get from your product. What is the current problem consumers face and how does it impact them? Explain the situation and relate it to something everyone can understand. Provide relevant examples that detail the problem, so your audience can identify with it. Then, provide a resolution. How does your product solve that problem? Focus on the benefits and not the features.

Your elevator pitch can also include a tagline, along with any unique information about your product. Discuss what differentiates your product or core values. Try using an association example to help the audience identify with your product. For instance, if you make high-end furniture you might say, "We're the Rolls Royce of sofas." Right away the audience associates luxury with your furniture. Use simple visuals to quickly give listeners a clear picture of what you do. At the end of your elevator pitch, the audience should be hooked and interested to learn more.

SLIDE STYLE

A common mistake is trying to fit too much information into your presentation. You have a tendency to want to demonstrate either how much you know or back up your points with tons of supporting information. Too much information can have a negative effect on the presentation. It is easier for the audience to get off message or lose track of your key points. Good investor presentations stick to a simple 10:20:30 rule. 10 Slides, 20 minutes long, using 30-point font.

Limit your presentation to 10 slides. All the information you need will fit onto those. Each slide should contain a new set of information and keep the pitch moving smoothly. Here is an example of slide titles I like, but feel free to create your own.

- **Title** – Title of the presentation, your name, company name, logo, tagline

- **Problem** – Describe the problem first. What's wrong with current products and how does that impact consumers? Why aren't existing products meeting their needs? Detail the issues and what it means for customers.

- **Solution** – Introduce your product. Discuss the value it brings. How does it solve the problem you have just outlined? How are customers better off with your product, what are the benefits, and why will they buy it? Give a detailed enough description, so the audience knows what your product does. Remember to focus on the benefits.

- **How You Make Money** – This is probably one of the most important pieces of information to investors, yet I've seen many presentations that almost completely leave this out. As an investor, I want to know how you plan to make money. Simple as that. On this slide, provide your business model. Discuss where you get your customers, how you make sales, and what kind of margins you have. Keep it simple and make it clear. If the audience is confused about where your revenue comes from, you've lost them.

- **Differentiation** – Describe what makes your product unique and different from other products.

How will your product stand out to customers? What will make them buy it? Do you plan to advertise this? If a technical feature differentiates you and is important to consumers, you can mention it here. Don't dwell too much on technical specs, but any patents or design features can also go on this slide. Make certain to relate any features back to benefits and describe how this differentiates you.

- **Marketing Plan** – This is the 10 Customer Plan approach. Describe how you will you reach your first 10 customers, then the next 100, then the next 1,000. Do not mention a shotgun approach and capturing a certain percentage of the market. You'll instantly lose credibility with investors. Include an overview of the marketing plan you have already written. Obviously, you can't squeeze your entire marketing plan onto one slide; please don't try. Just provide the important points on the slide and then you can discuss them in detail during the presentation.

- **Competition** – This slide is a great opportunity to break up the text and use graphics or logos for your competition. If you created a competitor graph in chapter 2, that's an excellent way to show whom your competitors are, their position in the market, and how you compare to them. Be prepared to discuss your competitors, their price points, their marketing strategies, target market, and success rate. Point out any opportunities your competitors may be missing, why that is, and how you plan to take advantage of them.

- **Management Team** – This is your opportunity to sell the investors on your team. Introduce each co-founder or executive member of your company. List their industry experience, accomplishments, and the expertise they bring. In addition, list any board of directors and their qualifications on this slide. Not only do investors consider the impact of your product, but also the experience of your team. Investors want to be confident with whom they are investing. A well-rounded team with industry experience will reflect well on your potential success.

- **Financial Plan** – This is a critical element of your presentation, and often where investors determine if your company is for real or not. Provide a basic one & three-year financial plan on this slide. You have already created a one-year projection for your sales plan. Extend that out to a three-year plan as well and include both charts. Clearly show income, expenses, projected profit, and the money you are requesting.

Be prepared to discuss any assumptions you have made, market factors, changing consumer buying patterns, internal and external forces, and other financial impacts. Investors love to quiz you on your assumptions and throw 'what if' questions at you. They want to see how realistic your figures are and how they hold up, based on their knowledge.

Investors look at figures all day long and have seen plenty of income statements to determine if you're being realistic or not. If you report a $5 million income after the second year, then you'd better be ready to show how you are going to get that. Present figures from the 10 customer approach and not the shotgun approach.

Don't you dare tell an investor that under ideal conditions, you can capture 1% of the market and that relates to $5 million in sales. Instead, describe how you will get your first 10 customers, then the next ones, and so on until you reach $5 million in sales. If you have questions on preparing financial statements, there are plenty of good resources online.

- **Status and Timeline** – Your closing slide will present the current status of your product and the timeline required to meet your goals. Is your product still in the development stage with a year needed to get it market ready, or is it already on the market? Give the investor an honest assessment of your product and any deadlines or time goals you have set. Let them know what they are getting into.

There are your 10 slides for the presentation. They give a complete overview of your product, strategy, market, competitors, and team. Most importantly, you've told the investors how you're going to make money and increase their investment. Your goal now is to complete this presentation in 20 minutes - any longer and the pitch seems to drag on. A good presentation is to the point and covers all the important information in less than 20 minutes. At the end of your presentation, invite questions from the audience. Make sure to allow for some Q&A time. I recommend keeping your slide show to 12-15 minutes, allowing 5-8 minutes of questions at the end. Relate any answers to your audience with examples and benefits they can understand. If you find yourself discussing technology or manufacturing processes, describe how that relates to the benefits. Which of these two statements is more impactful to an audience?

> *Our headphones have the new Z3 audio technology with an unbelievable audio range of 20 to 20,000 Hz. Three separate processing chips are used to achieve this range. Our headphones are made in a state-of-the-art Japanese factory, using a multi-indexed sound encoding process and shipped to our stores for resale. There's nothing like them on the market.*

> *Our headphones are made with the new Z3 audio technology, improving the audible range and enhancing sound quality. You can hear higher highs and lower lows. Manufacturing them in Japan not only saves us 20% in manufacturing costs, but we're also able to utilize the latest sound encoding processes vital to producing such a high quality sound. Our new headphones provide better sound clarity and quality over other headphones on the market.*

Do you see how matching technology with the benefits improves the relevance? The second statement is more impactful to a consumer. Practice the presentation in front of friends or family, until you have it dialed in. Make changes on the content, based on their feedback. If your friends are unclear on the material, then chances are the investor will be also. Time yourself to practice the pace and flow of the presentation. You do not want to appear rushed or flustered.

Use a 30-point font or larger for your slides. The slides need to be clear and legible from a distance. Your goal is to present the idea on the slide and then discuss it in your presentation. Do not try to write all of your information on the slide. Too much information and the slide will appear cluttered and confusing. 30-point font will ensure you only write the title and give the slides a clean image. If you present in a large room, you will want people in the back to be able to read your slides also. Use a 30-point font for a professional look and avoid any problems. Following the 10:20:30 rule is the key to building a successful investor presentation.

Finally, anticipate questions your audience may have. Try to address them in the presentation or be ready to answer them. If you have a new technology, people will naturally be unfamiliar with it. Take the time to look at this from the audience's perspective. If you had 20 minutes to understand this new technology, what would you want to hear? It's easy for entrepreneurs to forget this simple principle.

I will always remember a pitch I was given by a bio-lab company. The two owners had developed a new allergy testing process to replace the standard patch test people get from doctors. Their test was more accurate, less invasive, cost less, and offered a clear benefit. They could have listed just those four items on a slide for a compelling presentation. Instead, they spent 20 minutes discussing the science behind the test. All of their slides were full of laboratory terms and complex diagrams. By the end of the presentation, all of us had glazed looks in our eyes. Not only were we confused with the process, but we didn't know where to begin with questions. They had a great product, but failed to communicate any of the benefits or consider who their audience was. Their presentation only confused us further. Don't let this happen to you. Spend the time to create a meaningful presentation.

PREPARE FOR THE WORST

The first investor pitch I ever made was to a state-run small business loan fund for NaturelEyes. Each year they received funds from the state to invest in local start-ups. We sent our application and business plan to the committee and, after several anxious weeks, we finally received an appointment to present. We were instructed to keep the presentation brief, as there would be Q&A time at the end and that each committee member had read our business plan. We worked on the presentation for weeks. When the day finally arrived, we were all excited and prepared to impress. We even brought in a member from our board of directors to answer industry-specific questions. We had this money locked up.

Our presentation focused mainly on product features, what made us unique in the cosmetic market, and current favorable market trends. Our business plan was very detailed about pricing strategy, marketing, competitors, market position, and financial models, so we did not spend much time discussing those items. We assumed that each committee member had read our business plan and had a complete understanding of our company. If they had questions, we could discuss them during the Q&A.

Our secret weapon was the NaturelEyes product itself. People who tried the wrinkle reducer loved it so far. We planned a demonstration for committee members to try our product and experience it for themselves. Feeling the product in action was better than any slide show.

The problem was the committee consisted of nine men and one woman. Not only did 90% of them have no personal experience with cosmetics, but only one of them were willing to try the product. Our presentation was irrelevant because it focused on features these men didn't care about. The next problem was that only two of the committee members had actually read our business plan. For the other eight members, our presentation was the only information they had. We did not provide enough detail on key points for them to even ask questions. Finally, the presentation before us ran long so our time was cut by five minutes, only allowing for three questions at the end. Our morale went from sky high to bottomed out in 15 minutes.

I got the call the following day that we did not receive the funds. We had failed to demonstrate a profitable sales strategy or significant product value to the committee. We based our presentation on several assumptions that turned out to be false. Had we followed the 10:20:30 rule, we would have been much more prepared. Don't assume anything and always make sure to emphasize the important information. If questions aren't being asked, then ask the committee members questions instead. Unfortunately, we learned a hard lesson and wasted a lot of time in the process. Prepare for the worst case scenario and don't leave anything to chance.

17

BUSINESS PLANS ARE A WASTE OF TIME

Write A Great Plan With Little Effort

The only time you'll need a business plan is when you're applying to a VC or Angel Group for capital. Even then, investors know the numbers will change within the first six months anyway. I personally feel business plans are requested by investors as more of a test to see if you can put a meaningful one together. Otherwise, you'll never use them. They are more formal versions of your sales and marketing plans. The reason not many entrepreneurs use business plans any more is because they are lengthy and time consuming to write. You are going to have your hands full with daily challenges and issues as it is. You don't need another distraction trying to elaborately describe your business. Plus, nobody wants to take the time to read a 50-page plan for every startup business they come across. That wastes time too.

Every entrepreneur knows that things change frequently. As market conditions change, so do your forecasts and strategies. Numbers can have dramatic swings with just a few little changes in the market. Business plans aren't flexible enough to keep up with the ups and downs of a startup. What's the point of taking weeks to write something that will probably change in a month anyway? I believe it's better to figure things out as you go and consistently re-evaluate your plan along the way. A well-written sales plan will be more valuable during your first few years. Business plans simply highlight your company under ideal circumstances, when revenue is flowing and bank accounts are full, and not when you are strapped for cash.

So what good is a business plan? They force you to think about every aspect of your company in depth. They can help you see the complete picture and organize your company more efficiently. A nice business plan will also help you with investors and improve your chances of finding new capital. Writing a good business plan is still a useful skill for small business owners to have. Therefore, I'll show you how to write an impressive business plan using minimal effort and time. A great business plan is not a mystery.

I have read hundreds of business plans in the past few years and found the most impressive ones share a few fundamentals. The good plans always stand out right away, because they are well organized and easy to read. Unfortunately, not many business owners know how to write a good business plan and it ends up reflecting poorly on them. I've picked some of the best styles and formats from well-written business plans to share with you. I'll show you how to write an impressive plan that will stand out to investors. With a little luck, you can get through this quickly and get back to the more important requirements of running a business.

Write your business plan as if you are painting a picture of your company. Even though investors will see it, this is not a sales pitch. Your business plan is simply an accurate description of the workings, operations, and strategy of your business. Most of the information for the plan is going to be pulled right from the sales plan, marketing plan, and competitor analysis that you've already written. Pull those plans out and have them ready. The biggest challenge is organizing it properly. Lucky for you, I'm here to do the dirty work.

Next, determine whom you're presenting this plan to. Is it for a VC, Angel Investor, bank, peer-to-peer, or another investor type? This will determine how you focus the business plan. Include relevant information that investors will want to see. Anticipate any questions they may have and be sure to address them right in the plan. Research any additional information you need to support your strategies and forecasts. There is plenty of market data available online, so spend some time researching your information while you put this plan together. Also, create graphs and charts from this data to support your conclusions. They help to break up the pages, add interest, and can be valuable to support your strategy. Microsoft Excel makes it incredibly easy to create professional-looking graphs quickly. A few relevant graphs are a great way to add quality content to your plan. Finally, make sure to include your mission and vision in this plan. Use this plan to represent your personality and the goals that you want to set. Convey that personality to the audience.

Here is a simple, yet effective, outline for a business plan. It provides a well-organized and complete description of your company. You'll notice each main category is broken out into it is own component. Simply fill all the research and information you've already collected so far into each section. I've listed several topics you'll want to include in each category, but you're certainly not limited to these. Add any additional information necessary to your business. Provide enough detail for the reader to gain a complete understanding of each topic. Your goal is to accurately describe every aspect of your operation. It can be useful to elaborate on any technology, patents, or manufacturing detail relevant to your product. If it gives you a competitive advantage include it. However, assume the reader has no prior understanding of your industry or technology. Be sure to describe any technical information you include in layman's terms and relate it to a benefit.

OVERVIEW OF YOUR BUSINESS PLAN

1. **COVER PAGE**
   - Company name
   - Date
2. **TABLE OF CONTENTS**
3. **EXECUTIVE SUMMARY**
   - Business Concept and Description
   - Opportunity
   - Target Market
   - Strategy
   - Competitive Advantages
   - Management Team
   - 1-year financial forecast
4. **COMPANY & PRODUCT OVERVIEW**
   - Concept
   - The Product
   - Product Development Stage
   - Breadth and Depth of Product Line
   - Market Entry Strategy
   - Opportunity
5. **INDUSTRY ANALYSIS**
   - Target Market
   - Consumer Demographics

- Market Size
- Current
  Economic
  Forces
- Trends

6. COMPETITIVE ANALYSIS

- Competitors
- Breadth &
  Depth Analysis

7. CUSTOMER ANALYSIS

- Buying
  Patterns
- Purchasing
  Power
- Current
  Favorable

8. MARKETING & SALES STRATEGY

- Marketing Plan
- Sales Plan
- Positioning
- Pricing
- Product
- Placement

- SWOT Analysis
- Barriers To
  Entry
- Opportunity

- Market
  Position
  Analysis
- Substitute
  Products

Economic
Factors
- Opportunity
- Competitive
  Advantage

- Promotion
- Advertising
  Plan
- Customer
  Retention
- Milestones

9. OPERATIONS PLAN

- Manufacturing
- Distribution
- Facilities
- Overhead / Costs
- Regulatory Requirements
- Sustainability Issues

10. MANAGEMENT TEAM

- Executive Team
- Organization / Structure
- Compensation
- Board Of Directors
- Shareholders
- Stock Options & Bonus Plans

11. FINANCIAL PLAN

- Income Statement
- Balance Sheet
- One Year Pro Forma Statement
- Three Year Pro Forma Statement
- Assumptions
- Projections
- Cash Flow Analysis
- Break Even Chart
- Funding Requested

12. APPENDIX
- Charts & Graphs
- Data
- Resumes
- Collateral

The Executive Summary should be a one-page overview of your company to give the reader everything they need in a quick glance. Executive summaries are used quite often, because they provide on one page a detailed overview of the company, executive team, opportunity, and strategy. Many investors will initially ask to read your executive summary first instead of the full business plan. Read a few executive summaries online to find a style that fits your style.

When you do need to finally create a formal business plan, subscribe to LivePlan. For $19/month, their software easily creates a professional and detailed business plan. All of the financials are auto-calculated from simply entering your sales forecasts, including Profit & Loss statements and Cash Flows. They even provide examples for writing each section.

I hope that gives you enough information to write a simple and impressive business plan. Beyond investors, you won't find a lot of use for them. I believe you'll find your sales and marketing plans to be more useful and relevant. They can quickly be updated and adapted to changing market conditions. Business plans are just a little too long for practical use. It's a good idea to pull them out every six months to keep them updated. Otherwise, don't spend too much time on obsessing over the details. Save your time for more important issues.

18

HOW MUCH EQUITY SHOULD YOU GIVE AWAY

What Your Company Is Really Worth

So, the investor makes you an offer. Congratulations. Now the hard part comes. You need to figure out what a fair equity share is. How much of your company should you give away? How much is their investment really worth? Most entrepreneurs don't know the real value of their business and investors can take advantage of that. You need to know the value of your company, in order to determine a fair equity trade. This is known as a Pre-Money Valuation. Without it, you are taking a guess and giving more leverage to the investor. Believe me that they are hoping to get as much of your company as they can for their investment. You need to calculate your Pre-Money Valuation and determine an appropriate equity share to give up. Otherwise, you are taking a huge gamble and could end up losing.

Pre-Money Valuation is the value of your company before any outside investments are made. It determines how much equity the investment is worth. For example, if your company is worth $900,000, then a $100,000 investment would receive a 10% equity share. $900,000 + $100,000 = $1 million. $100,000 / $1 million = 10%. The Post-Money Valuation, the new value after the investment is made, is now $1 million. Make sense? We'll go through more examples.

Pre-Money Valuations are often difficult to calculate because they can be based on intangible items, such as sweat equity, intellectual property, and potential earnings. Hard money actually invested and sales are not the only factors. Entrepreneurs invest a lot of blood, sweat, and tears into their business, so the emotional attachment naturally raises your estimated value. Investors want the Pre-Money Value to be as low as possible, so their investment is worth more. They will try to rely on tangible measurements, such as existing money invested and sales. The trick is to build a case for your intangible items and support it with a solid sales strategy to reach your goals. Your goal is to convince the investors that your figures are achievable, in order to obtain the highest and realistic Pre-Money Value possible. Your business plan and negotiation skills will be put to the test.

Pre-Money Valuations can drastically vary by the size, type, product line, and industry of the startup. Unfortunately, there's no one single formula that says your company is worth this much. There are, however, several in depth and free calculators online I like. These are simple and easy to use calculators. Based on your responses to their questionnaire, they will provide an estimate of your Pre-Money Value. My recommendation is to be completely honest with your answers. If you're not sure, then choose the more conservative answer. It's easy to want to overestimate your value, but this isn't helpful when sitting in front of the investors. Use these calculators to give you an estimate of your current value and make any adjustments as needed.

Remember, these calculators are simply informational tools, and should be used only for educational purposes. They are meant to demonstrate popular qualifying criteria investors may consider. These are, by no means, meant to reflect what investors will actually value your company at, and a brief questionnaire may not accurately describe your company. I'm telling you to be smart and use these tools with common sense.

NAME	WEB ADDRESS
CAYENNE CONSULTING	www.caycon.com/valuation.php
OWN YOUR VENTURE	www.ownyourventure.com/equitySim.html
VENTURE CHOICE	www.venturechoice.com/calculators.htm

So you have an idea of what your company is worth. You know your Pre-Money Value. Here are the two formulas you'll use:

POST-MONEY VALUE = (PRE-MONEY VALUE) + (INVESTMENT AMOUNT)

INVESTMENT % = (INVESTMENT AMOUNT) / (POST-MONEY VALUE)

Add the proposed investment amount to your Pre-Money Value. This gives you a total value after the investment. This is called your Post-Money Value. Then divide the investment amount by your Post-Money Value. This is the equity percentage the investor could fairly ask for based on what your company is worth. Let's look at some examples:

Your Pre-Money Value is $400,000. The investor says they'll give you $125,000 for 30% in your company. Is this a fair offer?

Let's plug in the numbers. Post-Money Value = $400,000 + $125,000 = $525,000. A fair equity percentage for this investment is $125,000 / $525,000 or 23.8%.

The investor is asking for a higher than expected amount and the owner would be wise to counter at 24-25% or ask the investor to take on more responsibility for a 30% equity share.

This brings us to the topic of dilution. Share dilution is when your ownership in the company or equity percentage is reduced. If you have formed as a corporation, then you have issued shares in return for investment. As you bring on more investors, that percentage of ownership decreases. Therefore, your share is diluted. Say that you own 100% of the company and give yourself 1,000 shares. You bring on an investor and give him a 50% equity share. Now, you have 500 shares and he has 500 shares. You own 50% and he owns 50%. Or you may choose to increase the number of shares issued. You keep your 1,000 shares, issue another 1,000 shares to him, and there are now 2,000 shares in the company. You still own 50% and he still owns 50% with 1,000 shares each.

Share dilution can get a little complicated, because there are several ways to do it when you bring on new investors. The main point is to consider how much your share will actually get diluted. You may need more than one round of investment and bring on more investors over time. What happens to your share then, when you have three or four investors? This is very important to consider before giving away too much the first round.

We'll use your company from the example above to demonstrate equity dilution. You started the company by yourself and built it up to a Pre-Money Valuation of $400,000. Not bad. You bring on an investor and they agree *to invest $125,000 for a 24% equity share. That is round 1 of investing.*

One year later, sales are going well and you need to expand facilities. It will cost another $100,000 for a new factory space and equipment. This time your Pre-Money Valuation has grown to $900,000. What does this mean for your investment and the initial investors equity share? This is round 2 of investing.

Finally, one year later you go national. You open up stores across the country and decide to move your warehouse to a more central location. You need $250,000 to do this. Luckily your company has grown to a $2,000,000 Pre-Money Value. How much is your share worth before and after this third round of investing?

I've included a spreadsheet that outlines this example, so you can see how the equity shares change. Notice you go from 100% ownership to 61% ownership after only three rounds of investing. Each round your share decreases significantly. If you need to take on another round of investing, you could lose controlling share of the company.

Investment Rounds				
Round 1 Investment				$125,000
Round 2 Investment				$100,000
Round 3 Investment				$250,000
Pre-Money Value				
Round 1				$400,000
Round 2				$900,000
Round 3				$2,000,000
Post-Money Value				
Round 1				$525,000
Round 2				$1,000,000
Round 3				$2,250,000

Equity Shares	Start Up	Round 1	Round 2	Round 3
Ownership %	100%	76%	69%	61%
Investor 1 %	0%	24%	21%	19%
Investor 2 %	0%	0%	10%	9%
Investor 3 %	0%	0%	0%	11%

This is a simple example to show how your share can quickly get reduced. It's important to understand dilution when seeking new capital. It is smart to anticipate future investments and what they can mean for your company. It is easy to jump at your first investment offer, but failing to plan for the future now can leave you in a difficult situation later. Take time to research Pre- and Post-Money Values, along with Equity Dilution. There are plenty of great resources available online to show you exactly how to calculate these, when you're ready.

When you walk in to meet with investors, have this information ready to go. It will impress them that you accurately understand Pre- and Post-Money Valuation. You'll also be able to negotiate a fair investment amount, knowing exactly how much you should give up. If you are not comfortable with their offer, discuss your reasons why with them. It is okay to turn the investor's offer down. It shows that you're a savvy entrepreneur who wants the best for his company. If you are not getting the best deal, don't be afraid to walk away. Only accept an offer if you are 100% comfortable with it and have run the calculations for your Pre- and Post-Money values.

Knowing this information gives you more leverage in the negotiation process. The old saying of 'don't bring a knife to a gunfight holds true.' Know what you're walking into and prepare accordingly. When your negotiations come to within 5% of what you were hoping to receive, then consider that a good deal. Investors like to play hardball, so don't haggle over every penny or decimal point. With a few negotiating skills and the numbers to back you up, you can make certain to get the best deal.

19

THE MORAL AND ETHICAL DILEMMA

Should You Want To Make Money?

You produce economic (low priced) coffee makers and distribute all over the United States. Sales have been good in your first year and you've sold over 10,000 units. One day you receive an email from your engineers that some of the thermostat are faulty. In your quest to keep costs low, you chose a lower quality thermostat that has been shown to fail about 5% of the time. The result from the bad thermostat is the heating element gets too hot, which melts the plastic casing and can cause the machine to catch fire. Of the 10,000 units you've sold, potentially 500 units may have this faulty thermostat. The cost of the recall would be about $40 per unit with advertising, shipping, and a refund. That's a $400,000 expense to try and fix 500 units. You simply can't afford that in your first year. However, you also know that your target market is primarily younger buyers who may have the coffee maker in dorm rooms or crowded apartments. The chance of a fire spreading could be disastrous. What should you do? What is your responsibility?

This scenario is not far from a real event that actually happened. It highlights the difficult decisions you will be faced with as a business owner. One decision benefits you financially and could greatly impact your revenue. The other decision helps to protect possible harm on your customers and could affect your company image. You will often be faced with decisions that have both a positive and negative result. Recall the coffee makers and you put your company at financial risk - not to mention the potential damage to branding. Choose not to recall the coffee makers and you risk your customer's safety and lives. Which one should you choose? What is your moral responsibility?

This is often a hotly contested issue. Is a business in business simply to make money? Is that the sole purpose of a business? Or are businesses obligated to step in and either stop harmful actions or prevent further damage from occurring? Should a business be held responsible for moral decisions? There are clear and well-backed arguments for both sides. Every year, we see examples of companies making these types of decisions. In 2012, Toyota recalled 7.43 million cars[1] with a power window problem that could lead to fire. They chose to prioritize their

[1] Charles Riley, *Toyota Recalls 7.43 Million Cars* (CNN Money, October 10, 2012)

customer's safety. British Petroleum allowed loose regulations that eventually led to the worst oil spills in United States' history. They chose to favor their revenue and bottom line. These decisions cost businesses millions of dollars. It will be your decision as a business owner to make that choice for your company. You will be responsible for the moral compass your business follows. How will you set your policies?

After years of being a business owner and having faced these decisions myself, I have debated this issue at length over the past 10 years. From all the examples and information presented, I reached a conclusion about a company's moral responsibility. I based it on placing your company in the best position to succeed and practice sustainable business. This means balancing risks and following strategies that allow you to operate long term. I challenge you to think about this issue as well and form your opinion. If your goal is creating a sustainable business, how does that shape your moral strategy? Does it change the way you operate overall? Your answer to this question can impact your operations. Spend some time to think about this.

I believe the answer is simple. A business is in business to make money. That's what a business does. The company has a responsibility to itself to create sustainable practices, in order to increase its value. This means the company needs to engage in activities and create products that are beneficial to their revenue. That is their only responsibility.

While businesses are made up of people, the business itself is not a person, so therefore can't be responsible for moral or immoral decisions. The people making decisions are either moral or immoral. That is a culture issue. Businesses are simply profitable or not profitable.

Businesses are also part of a community. Their geographic location, customer base, and industry are all communities the business belongs to. In order to engage in sustainable business, the company must support its community. Without customers, there is no business. If they are creating a product or event that is knowingly and directly harmful to its community, then they must take action to prevent it. Let me repeat that. If the company creates a product or event that knowingly and directly harms its consumers or community, then it is their responsibility to take action and prevent it.

Allowing harmful activities to happen hurt your sustainability and will eventually decrease your revenue. Lawsuits, bad publicity, public outcry, tougher regulations, and damaged branding are all possible results of harmful actions. When companies are found negligent, the consequences can be severe. These results go against the one purpose of the company. So, it is their responsibility to support the economic health of their community and customer base, in order to create revenue. That is a business' only true obligation.

Let me tell you the rest of the real story about that coffeemaker. In 1989, in Salt Lake City, Utah and in a home not far from mine, a family set their coffeemaker to turn on at 6 AM. While heating up both the thermostat and cutoff fuse malfunctioned[2]. Instead of the coffee maker turning off, it got hotter. The plastic melted and the coffeemaker caught fire. The fire spread so quickly through the home, that the homeowner was unable stop the fire. He called 911, and went upstairs to evacuate his family. Within minutes the smoke and flames made it impossible for him to reach his sleeping children. His 4-year-old son and a 14-year-old family friend sleeping over were killed. Their 6-year-old daughter was also badly burned. I remember this incident well, because the 14-year-old family friend killed was a classmate of mine in junior high. It is a real reminder of the responsibility businesses have to consumers.

If you were the CEO of this coffeemaker what would you do based on this principle? Your responsibility is to create sustainable business practices, and in our example spending $400,000 on a full recall would significantly hurt that pursuit. However, you are also knowingly creating a harmful product that can directly hurt your customer base. It would damage your community, instead of help it. You are obligated to take action, in order to prevent it. A possible solution is to issue repair notices

---

[2] Elaine Jarvik, *Total Recall: Haunting Memories* (Deseret News: December 27, 1991)

and operation warnings. Notify customers that a faulty thermostat can create a fire hazard and you have shipped new thermostats to repair outlets around the country. They can either take their coffeemaker to the outlet for repair or return it for a refund. The notice could also include a warning to place the coffeemaker in a safe place and operate under supervision, in order to prevent accidents. You have taken action to correct the problem, protected your customers from potential harm, and supported your community for future revenue. While these actions will still cost money, it is a more efficient solution that satisfies your responsibility.

This debate is sure to continue for many years. People will always have different opinions on the moral responsibility of a business. There may not be a perfectly definitive answer. These are important questions to ask yourself though. You must be prepared to act, when faced with such dilemmas. I challenge you to act in the best interests of your company and your community.

20

BUILD YOUR EMPIRE

How To Handle Growth

Y ou've made it to the last chapter of the book. For those of you still determined to start your own business, I have one final piece of advice for you. *Handle your growth slowly and smartly.* As you start to see revenue increase, you will feel the urge to expand. It is a normal feeling that drives you to want more. If you are making a little in one market, then you assume that you can make a lot in many markets. This thinking will often get you in trouble and can lead to failure pretty quickly. You need to take the right steps during expansion and maintain a solid foundation. When you feel it is time to grow, be careful with your plans and don't take on more than you can handle. Here are several tips to determine if you're ready to expand.

- Have you shown a steady and consistent growth in <u>profits</u> over the past 12 months? Increased profits show you're increasing sales, while maintaining steady operating costs. If your revenue and costs are both increasing each month, so your profits are the same, that only means you are maintaining a margin. You need to show controlled operating costs and consistent profits before expanding into new markets.

- Do you have the resources to expand? Will you hire new people or do you simply expect people to take on more work and responsibility? Consider the new workload you're adding and don't forget to account for adding additional resources to get it done. A common mistake is that business owners assume they will be able to handle the new workload themselves. This creates a serious time strain and ends up hurting your business overall, not to mention family. Existing accounts are neglected and may leave. New accounts don't get the full attention they require. Be careful not to overextend yourself when expanding. It is easy to do and will hurt your business. Be prepared to expand your resources as well and consider that cost first. If you expect $50,000 in revenue from this new market, but it will require hiring two full time people at $60,000, then the expansion probably isn't worth it right now.

- Examine current trends, economic factors, customer behavior, and buying power in the new market to see if you can expect the same success as your current market. Small changes in your target market or geographic location can yield dramatically different results. For example, having a high-end clothing store on the Miracle Mile in downtown Chicago is quite different than placing it just five miles away in a lower income suburb. Ensure that the community properly supports your business model, so that you will have staying power in the new location. You don't want to spend all your time and money on a new location, only to realize it's not profitable and needs to be closed down. Spend time researching the perfect location or new market, based on your ideal demographics.

- Make certain any systems, trainings, or processes are fully transferable to the new location. Take a look at your core operations and what makes it run so smoothly. Are you able to duplicate those processes in the new location? Everything that made you successful so far will need to be brought to the new location.

- Prepare a new sales and marketing plan for the new location. You'll want to fully evaluate all the economic factors and forces that impact your sales. Approach the new market, just like you did the first market. Do plenty of research and due diligence. Your strategy may be the same as before or it may be different. Build a completely separate plan for the new market.

- Get familiar with any new regulations or requirements in the new market. Do they require different labeling information, do they have different registrations you need, or are there any local laws that may affect your business? Fully examine any new requirements that you need to meet, in order to do business in the new market.

- Finally, how does your intellectual property transfer to the new market? Is there any issue with your name or logo? Do a quick trademark and name search in your new market for any problems you may run into. Also, are there any cultural differences that could impact your business operations? Does your name, logo, or tagline have a different meaning in the new market than your current one? For example, in the United States the thumbs-up gesture is very positive and indicates good job. However, in Thailand it's a very obscene gesture. Make sure your business isn't making any unknown blunders in the new market.

As you grow, do not take the decision to expand lightly. There are many factors to consider before making that step. Make sure the timing is right, the market is ready, and you will have staying power once you do expand. Take care of your money. It's easy to spend to your limits, meaning you will want to spend the money as fast as you earn it. That's a common mistake that ends up hurting business owners. It is okay to save your profits, build up a buffer, and wait for the right opportunity to come along. How you handle your growth will determine if you are around for a long time or just another business that doesn't make it past five years.

GOOD LUCK

The Conclusion

Starting a business is incredibly difficult. It requires an enormous amount of effort, determination, and creativity. My fifteen years of startups and running businesses have been an amazing journey – an adventure that I had always wanted. Those years have been filled with joy that comes from building your dreams into reality, and seeing your hard work payoff. They have also been filled with frustration, anxiety, heart-break and despair. It's not easy being an entrepreneur. There isn't any safety net for when you fall. There isn't paid-time off, a 401(k), 9-to-5 hours, or any consistency many people value in their lives. I want you to understand what you are getting yourself into. I urge you to think very carefully about starting a business before actually doing it. I then urge you to take that leap with confidence and determination.

For a select few of you, starting your own business will be one of the best things you have ever done in your life. Your reward will be the success of knowing you took a chance and followed your passions. You will feel the joy of taking your idea and building it into an actual product – the sheer elation from seeing your product on store shelves for the very first time. For you, there is no better feeling than making your own way in life and being an entrepreneur.

In this book, I have given you the tools required to start your own business with confidence. I hope you take away the knowledge and understanding to make your business successful. My goal was to make this a complete and easy-to-follow guide for all entrepreneurs. I wanted to share my personal experiences and solutions, while running a business. I know that the challenges I have faced will not be very different from the difficulties and barriers you will also face. The ideas and techniques presented in this book will help you overcome those obstacles. I'm confident you will be successful with the knowledge I have shared with you.

Writing this book has been its own adventure, because it has made me reflect on many of my experiences and remember what it was like to struggle with these challenges. It has also forced me to examine my current practices and improve upon them. During the course of writing this, there were several opportunities that I realized I wasn't taking full advantage of. I found ways to improve and make several changes in my businesses to take advantage of those opportunities. The market will never stop changing, so your strategies need to keep improving too. Continually update your business model, sales plan, and marketing plan. Create your Simple Startup Guide to keep track of everything you do. Keep all of your plans, strategies, analysis, and charts in it, and refer back to your guide quarterly.

As your journey progresses, continue to evolve and build upon new opportunities.

Finally, share your story with other entrepreneurs. I challenge you to start a blog, website, or publication to share your ideas. Communicate with others and build your network. As an entrepreneur, you belong to a community of people, like yourself. We are here to support, encourage, and help you throughout this process. We also count upon you to support us in our ventures.

Simply starting a business is actually fairly easy. It is building your business the right way that is the challenge. I've given you the guide to do that - now it is up to you. How well you process this information will determine if you are able to avoid the common and costly mistakes waiting for you. Your customers are out there. They are always searching for better solutions to improve their lives. It's up to you to deliver that solution. You have the information to get started. You know how to reach your customers. You know how to build a successful marketing campaign. You know how to beat your competition. What's stopping you? If you use this information, I have confidence you will be successful. Go out there and get your first ten customers. With a little determination, I know that you will turn your idea into that next great thing.

Be Bold. Be Disruptive. Be Creative.
GOOD LUCK

For the latest tools, tips, and information from me visit

www.5hourmba.com

Check out my other startup resources and how-to guides online

Join me on Google+, LinkedIn or Facebook under 5-Hour MBA

Dedicated
To
Colin Farbotko

This book is dedicated to my long-time friend, Colin Farbotko. I met Colin our freshman year at Luther College in 1996. He was tall, athletic, artistic, funny, and played the guitar – every guy's nightmare trying to compete for girls' attention. Colin never accepted the normal boundaries of life. He was always creating something or pushing limits to see how far he could go. He was the first person I knew to create an online blog used for hilarious articles about life around campus, posting pictures and columns of his social life, and even using it as a voice when the college put pressure on him to stop his blog. He was years ahead of his time using social media.

Colin became well known in college for his time spent in the Art building casting bronze sculptures, his knowledge of Monty Python quotes, and complete disregard for public nudity laws. After college, he continued to create and built websites for a Fortune 50 company. His artistic creativity knew no bounds. It was also around this time he discovered his addiction for running triathlons. I often remember days when he would return from a 15-mile training run, make a sandwich and join me on the couch for an episode of the Simpsons, and then would hop up, proclaiming he was going out for another quick 10-mile run. In 2004, he completed his first Ironman Triathlon. I have never met anyone with the same drive that Colin had.

In 2006, Colin was diagnosed with ALS. Despite the aggressiveness of the disease, he never relented while fighting it. He continued to live his life to the fullest and never slowed down. He created another blog called, "I know it's sad, but I can't stop laughing." He fought ALS with humor, creativity, and persistence. Colin's courage was an inspiration to his family and friends. He inspired me to pursue my dreams, never fear challenges, and to believe that everything is possible. Taking a chance on starting new businesses and facing the risks of being an entrepreneur didn't seem as frightening anymore. In 2012, I went after one of my biggest dreams and signed up for my first triathlon. The months of training were exhausting, but I always kept Colin in my mind – pushing me further. On October 15, 2012, I completed my triathlon – finishing 31st overall and 3rd in my age group. Sadly, I never got to share the news with Colin. He quietly passed away that same morning.

You helped make this book possible. Thank you for your inspiration, courage, humor, laughter, and friendship.

You can read Colin's blog "I know it's sad, but I can't stop laughing" at:
http://colinfarbotko.blogspot.com/

Enjoy your Surly beer, my friend.